Genre,
TEXT,
grammar

PETER KNAPP is Director of Educational Assessment Australia and Associate Professor at the School of Education, University of New South Wales. He has worked in literacy education for many years and has written a range of books, articles and teaching materials on teaching and assessing writing.

MEGAN WATKINS is a Lecturer in Education at the University of Western Sydney. She has written a number of articles and curriculum materials on genre theory and literacy pedagogy.

Genre, TEXT, *grammar*

TECHNOLOGIES FOR TEACHING AND ASSESSING WRITING

PETER KNAPP

and

MEGAN WATKINS

A UNSW Press book

Published by
University of New South Wales Press Ltd
University of New South Wales
Sydney NSW 2052
AUSTRALIA
www.unswpress.com.au

National Library of Australia
Cataloguing-in-Publication entry

    Knapp, Peter, 1947– .
    Genre, text, grammar: technologies for teaching and
    assessing writing.
    Includes index.
    ISBN 0 86840 647 3.
    1. Language arts. 2. literary form – Study and teaching.
    I. Watkins, Megan. II. Title.
    372.6044

Design Di Quick
Print Everbest Printing

Contents

Foreword

BY GUNTHER KRESS

PROFESSOR OF ENGLISH, INSTITUTE OF EDUCATION, UNIVERSITY OF LONDON

The tasks of education are not becoming easier. In anglo-phone – therefore neo-liberal – societies, schools are forced into increasingly paradoxical situations of intense forms of surveillance and control by the State, in environments that are ever more fractured, fragmented and diverse. Economies have long since moved beyond the control of the State and the market is now the dominant force in society. So the two major tasks of schooling in a still quite recent past – the production of citizens and reproduction of labour – have become problematic or have begun to disappear. In the midst of this, schools, schooling and institutional education more generally have to find their own way.

Communication is marked by all these forces. Forms of writing are now deeply different to what they had been even 20 years ago, in grammar, syntax and in textual form; email and texting are changing levels of formality and thereby 'manners' of writing more quickly than anything else has done in the last century or two; the screen both imposes and makes possible entirely different forms of 'composing' and of reading; image and writing jostle for attention and supremacy on pages and on screens.

Teachers bear the brunt of these tensions, contradictions and insistent new demands. Like some other professionals, they seem ever more peculiar in their continuing commitment to those whom they serve. In our research in schools in London – and there would be no difference to this anywhere in Australia – whether in Science classrooms or those of English, one thing is absolutely clear: teachers want to do what is best for the young people in their classrooms. They want, by hook or by crook, to give them the best possible start in their adult, social and working lives.

One big difference between the teacher of Science and the teacher in the English classroom is precisely the matter of 'communication'. The ability to communicate fully in all important ways is the single most significant prerequisite for full participation in social, economic and cultural life. In an era when screens of all kinds are shunting the print media into lesser prominence, writing remains crucial. Yes, image has already displaced writing in many places in public communication, and yet writing remains the preferred form of the elites – economic, social, cultural and political. And writing is still the most important means of access to the vast repository of knowledge of literate cultures. Those facts alone demand that students in school should gain the fullest, deepest, and richest means of using the cultural technology of writing. Equity of access and full participation both rest on that.

But for that to be truly the case, teachers themselves need the resources that show what this technology is, how it works, how it can be used – whatever the purposes and aims of those who have need of it. Not all of them come to school with that knowledge, and certainly not all come with equal understanding. And so a sine qua non of equitable provision and outcomes is that this cultural resource must be available to all: clearly, openly, explicitly, with no mystifications of any kind.

That is what this book has set out to do; and it is what it provides. That is the aim of its authors. They have a vast store of experience to draw on, which shows everywhere, whether in the examples used or in their manner of setting forth their materials. I admire their hands-on, let's-get-this-job-done attitude: here are theorists who know what is needed, and practitioners who are clear about the need of real understanding. Both practical use and theory are set out in clear, yet rich detail.

Both authors have a well-earned reputation through the real usefulness of their work in precisely this area, not only in Australia, but in the UK, North America and South Africa. I am certain this book, which builds on their knowledge and experience in many ways, will be a constantly valued resource and a great success. It fully deserves to be both.

Introduction

Over the last 10 years there has been considerable change in literacy curriculum both in Australia and internationally. Genre-based approaches to writing, which emerged in Australia in the late 1980s, now underpin primary English syllabus documents in Australia, New Zealand, Singapore, Malaysia and Hong Kong. Genre-based approaches are far removed from the naturalistic models of language learning (Barnes, Britton and Rosen 1971; Krashen 1981, 1984) that framed approaches such as whole language (Smith 1975, 1983; Goodman 1986; Cambourne 1988) and process writing (Graves 1975, 1978, 1983; Walshe 1981a and b), which dominated the teaching of writing throughout the late 1970s and well into the 1990s. These progressivist approaches, closely aligned with Piagetian principles of developmental psychology, viewed language learning as essentially an individualised phenomenon and, as such, reacted against the formal instruction of grammar and textual form. Genre-based curricula place a strong emphasis on an explicit teaching of grammar and text, and their widespread adoption in recent years is testament to their effectiveness in improving students' literacy out-comes. To many teachers, however, who either attended school or received their teacher training when the naturalistic models of language learning prevailed, genre-based curriculum can be quite daunting, especially given its focus on the teaching of grammar. This book is designed to provide assistance to this generation of teachers who, in a sense, 'missed out' on learning about grammar and to act as a guide for the next generation of teachers in effective ways to program, implement and assess genre, text and grammar – what we consider to be the three key technologies for teaching writing.

In developing this genre, text and grammar approach we have drawn on a number of different theoretical perspectives of language and language learning. By and large, genre-based approaches to writing are based on a functional model of language; that is, a theoretical perspective that emphasises the social constructedness of language. The development of a functional approach in Australia is due first and foremost to the influence of M.A.K. Halliday (1978, 1985) whose work has sparked a wealth of applied research in language education well beyond the usual scope of applied linguistics. The approach that is followed in this book is indebted to Halliday's profound insights into the social aspects of literacy, although our work does not pretend to strictly follow systemic–functional linguistics. We have been similarly influenced by the work in critical linguistics and social semiotics of Gunther Kress (1982, 1985, 1989), who originally proposed the notion of *genre* as *social process*. We are also greatly indebted to the linguistic research in *genre theory* by J.R. Martin (1986, 1987, 1992) and Joan Rothery (1986). While the approach to genre, text and grammar that we have pursued is different in significant ways from their original work, we nevertheless would not have developed the *process/product* model of genre without it. The model for genre, text and grammar proposed in this book builds on our earlier work presented in *Context–Text–Grammar* (1994). In our work on genre, text and grammar, we have always attempted to make the ideas and theories that inform contemporary linguistics and semiotics relevant and accessible to classroom teachers. In our previous book, as here, we have been motivated first and foremost by our close contact with teachers and the demands made on them in their classrooms, rather than searching for a model compatible with the technicalities of recent linguistic and semiotic theories. We have tried, therefore, to understand the problems teachers and students face in understanding how language works, and have applied some useful theoretical positions towards solving some of those problems.

In this book we focus specifically on genre, text and grammar from a pedagogic perspective. While emphasis is given to the primary years of schooling, both our approach to genre and our cross-curriculum focus means this is a useful text for teaching writing well into the high school years and beyond. In Chapter 1 we provide a rationale and brief theoretical outline of the approach to language underpinning this book. It deals with each of the three technologies of writing we utilise in this approach: genre, text and grammar; different perspectives on each and why it is useful to have these categories in the teaching of writing. Chapter 2 is essentially a glossary of grammatical terms. It is designed as an easy reference explaining all the terms that are used within the genre-based grammar which we propose. The focus of Chapter 3 is the teaching of genre, text and grammar. It firstly provides an account of previous approaches to teaching writing, examining the shift from progressivist to genre-based methodologies. This is followed by an outline of the approach to teaching writing that we advocate, highlighting the four integrated elements of content/language, structure, grammar and assessment, and a set of key principles that we feel frames effective pedagogic practice. Chapters 4 to 8 then deal with the five fundamental genres of school writing: *describing, explaining, instructing, arguing* and *narrating*. In the first instance, each is described in terms of its distinctive grammar and textual structures. Each chapter proceeds to exemplify the teaching/learning of the grammatical and structural features of the genre through typical units of work. The final section of these chapters provides a diagnostic approach to assessing genre, text and grammar. We demonstrate how genre-specific criteria can identify strengths and weakness in typical pieces of student writing and suggest some practical strategies and interventions to address specified areas of need.

As indicated, our main objective in writing this book is to assist teachers in the difficult process of teaching their students how to write. While our focus is practice, we have tried to meld theory and practice in an approach with the clear pedagogic intent of equipping students with a generative set of knowledge and skills to both write effectively and to play knowingly with textual form.

Acknowledgments

The approach to genre and grammar used in this book was first developed for the New South Wales Metropolitan West Region Literacy and Learning Program, *Genre and Grammar Resource Materials*. Versions of each of the chapters on the genres of school writing first appeared in Knapp and Watkins (1994), but have been revised to include more detailed information on aspects of genre, text and grammar, and sections on a diagnostic approach to assessment. The teaching ideas in Chapter 5 – The Genre of Explaining – are drawn from *Far Out* by Watkins and Knapp (1998).

Gunther Kress (Institute of Education, University of London), Dr Helen Nicholls (Advisor, Ministry of Education, New Zealand), Greg Noble (School of Humanities, University of Western Sydney) and Robyn Mamouney (New South Wales Department of Education and Training) read and made significant editorial contributions to the text. Andrew Rolfe, previously Literacy and Learning Consultant to the Metropolitan West Region of the New South Wales Department of Education and Training, contributed to an early draft of Chapter

5. Also, Helen Pearson (Educational Assessment Australia, University of New South Wales) contributed to the strategies for assessing writing.

We are indebted to the following teachers – Jennifer McKeown, Fiona Ardus, Jane Brincat, Peter Bradshaw, Trish Haynes and Tanya Rose – for providing the opportunity to conduct research and work with students in developing the approach for use in infants and primary classrooms.

We are also appreciative of the support given by Marina and Alex Grant, Susan and Katy Green, Charlie Knapp, Louisa Mamouney, Jonathan Kress, Dee and Mitchell Horrocks, and Declan Noble. We would also like to acknowledge the support and assistance of Debbie Lee at UNSW Press.

CHAPTER 1

A GENRE-BASED MODEL OF LANGUAGE

The model of language outlined in this book is based on the view that language is processed and understood in the form of texts. A text can be any meaning-producing event, be it a book, a film, an advertisement, a phone conversation and so on. A text can be seen from two key perspectives: a thing in itself that can be recorded, analysed and discussed; and also a process that is the outcome of a socially produced occasion. Most people like to talk and think about texts as products, which is why the notion of a text type is quite prevalent in literacy studies. In this book, however, we focus our attention on the latter notion of text as a social process because we have found it to be a more productive and generative approach from the point of view of teaching students the core skills of literacy. In this chapter we will outline our theoretical perspective on texts and compare it with some of the more product-oriented notions of text.

HOW DO WE LEARN TO USE LANGUAGE?

Language is both natural and cultural, individual and social. Debates over the past 30 years have often polarised language into either natural or social domains. To treat such a fundamental human activity in this way is unproductive.

Progressivism, the dominant perspective on teaching language and literacy in the 1970s and 1980s, promoted language as an entirely natural individualistic phenomenon and thus relegated language learning to the personal domain. This created all sorts of problems for teachers. How can language be taught when it is totally within the private domain? The best that can be done is to foster its 'emergence' in individual students. Teaching became more like managing or facilitating, with 'learning experiences' planned in the hope that they would draw out the appropriate language. This process has maximum effect in only a limited number of cases; for many students it produces very little language development and effective learning.

As adults it is easy to think that our own facility with language is 'natural'; we simply can't imagine our everyday lives without it. Our knowledge and use of language and grammar operates at an implicit level; it appears to us to be neutral and unproblematic. In other words, our knowledge about language is transparent and this deceives us into thinking that there is nothing to know, or that whatever there is to know can be effortlessly 'picked up'.

There is also a view that learning to speak and learning to write are identical processes (Cambourne 1988, p. 45). Learning to speak is seen to be entirely natural – children acquire speech simply through immersion – a view that overlooks the immense teaching role played by parents and siblings (Painter 1991). Writing, so it follows in this view, can be acquired through a similar process of immersion in the written word. However, not only is the 'immersion view' totally implausible as an account of what actually happens, it is also the case that speech and writing have a fundamentally different organisation in structure, grammar, function and purpose (Halliday 1985). Immersing students in writing (whatever that could mean) for one or two hours a day is an inadequate teaching and learning strategy. Learning to write is a difficult and complex series of processes that require a range of explicit teaching methodologies throughout all the stages of learning.

Speech and writing are both forms of communication that use the medium of language, but they do so quite differently. It is usual to think that they are simply different aspects of the same thing; however, writing is far more than speech transcribed. For one thing, the fact that one is a visual form while the other exists in sounds has fundamental effects. The latter exists in time, the former less so. While it is true that the writing of young students is generally very speech-like, as they learn to write, it becomes less so. It is useful, therefore, to understand some of the basic differences between speech and writing.

A language operates both in time and space. Speech is first and foremost a time-based medium. Most forms of speech are interactions between people, in time: exchanging information or sequencing their descriptions of events and/or actions. From this point of view, speech can be described as temporal, immediate and sequential. Writing, on the other hand, is an inscription. It is language in a spatial medium. Writing takes language out of the constraints and immediacy of time and arranges it hierarchically. In informal, casual speech, clause follows clause, linked by conjunctions such as *so*, *then*, *and*, *but*, *when*, *because* and so on. Such speech is linked by the intonational means of the voice – like beads on a chain (Kress 1982). In writing we arrange clauses into a sentence: the main idea becomes the main clause; subsidiary ideas become subordinate clauses and so on (Hammond 1991). The logic of sequence becomes the logic of hierarchy. Also, we can edit writing – go back over our work and rearrange it on the page, whereas with speech we have to use fillers such as 'ums' and 'ahs' in order to help us 'think on our feet'. Writing makes greater use of the potential for language to be abstract, either through the process of nominalising clauses (changing processes/verbs into new nouns), for example:

We changed the tyre, and that made us late.

to

The changing of the tyre made us late.

or, through using verbs metaphorically.

Students play **sport** every Friday

compared with

Why do peacocks *sport* such outrageously resplendent plumage?

or

She was *sporting* an awful new haircut.

When teaching students to write in English, it is important for the teacher and the student to have a basic understanding of how English operates and functions as writing and the ways in which writing is substantially different from speech. When students first start to write, their attempts closely resemble their speech. Consider the types of writing students first learn to control; texts like recounts, which are formally similar to speech. Through the process of learning to write, however, students gradually move into the more abstract, hierarchical forms that are more typical of writing.

Equally problematic to the progressivist view that language is entirely natural is the socio-linguistic view that the ability to produce language is entirely social. Approaches to the teaching of writing that simply focus on the social too easily leave individuals and their autonomy completely out of the picture. They can appear to be too cold, hard and scientific. They leave no space for the individual writer and, moreover, are unable to deal with the creative potential of writing. In particular, they tend to reduce creative forms of writing, such as narrative, to structures and formulas. While such approaches may be effective in scientific writing, in narrative, poetic and literary writing they fall a long way short of the mark.

The genre, text and grammar model of language proposed here recognises that while language is produced by individuals, the shape and structure of the language is to a large degree socially determined. The implications of this for teachers are enormous. An extreme individualistic/creative view eliminates teaching; an extreme social/structuralist view eliminates the individual. The perspective on language as social process, however, allows us to explain and analyse arrangements of language (texts) as grammatical structures or constructions that are formed by individuals in social contexts to serve specific social needs and requirements.

In this view the language conventions which a child learns are considered to be substantially already 'in place', formed by the society into which he or she will move. Yet children, as is the case with any language-user, are constantly remaking the language they use as they require it. A young child who says 'Shut the light' is reshaping language. All language-users are in this position; we use an existing system for making our meanings, and in doing so we remake that system, if only in minute ways. From this point of view, language is constantly remade by those who use it; but in order to use it, we must first have some competence with it.

WHAT IS A GENRE, TEXT AND GRAMMAR MODEL OF LANGUAGE?

The genre, text and grammar model of written language proposed here is primarily concerned with 'what's going on' in writing; it asks why a particular type of writing works better than another. For example, if we are required to write a technical description, it is not helpful or indeed easy, in our culture, to use a narrative genre. We need to understand that technical descriptions have recognisable characteristics and that using these characteristics will make the writing process effective and efficient. Second, the textual conventions for technical descriptions will help readers to pick up the signals and read the text from a technical point of view. The textual characteristics of a story, on the other hand, would make the process cumbersome and inefficient, as well as giving readers the wrong reading signals.

The aim of a genre, text and grammar approach, then, is to provide students with the ability to use the codes of writing (the genres and grammar) effectively and efficiently. Without these codes the process of writing can be a frustrating and unproductive process. How many times do we see students staring at a blank piece of paper because they do not know how to start, let alone proceed with a writing task? A primary aim of teaching writing, therefore, is to provide students with the knowledge to become effective users of written English. The aim is not to provide students with simplistic formulas or rules and regulations for 'correct' English. While rules and formulas have their uses, on their own they do not produce powerful writers, writers who will become competent, confident and articulate users of the English language.

FOUR PERSPECTIVES ON LANGUAGE

CONTEXT

Texts are always produced in a context. While texts are produced by individuals, individuals always produce those texts as social subjects; in particular, social environments. In other words, texts are never completely individual or original; they always relate to a social environment and to other texts.

In the 1920s, the anthropologist Bronislaw Malinowski (1967) found it necessary to broaden the term 'context' in order to provide a fuller picture of what was going on around language. He coined the term 'context of situation' in order to have a way to describe the immediate environment in which texts are produced. He found, however, that this category did not account for the broader influences on texts and therefore developed the term 'context of culture' to describe the system of beliefs, values and attitudes that speakers bring with them into any social interaction.

One of the key theoretical linguists in the development of a functional model of language, Halliday (1978, 1985), proposed a highly articulated relationship between context and text. Context, or what is going on around a language event, is seen as 'virtual' or having the potential to 'actualise' the event in the form of a text. Halliday developed a specific terminology in order to describe these relationships or correspondences between context and text. For example, the content or stuff being talked or written about in the context is actualised in the text as 'ideational' or 'representational' meaning, the social relations between the participants in the context are actualised in the text in terms of 'interpersonal' meaning, and finally, the mode or medium of the language event is actualised in the text as 'textual' meaning.

Examples of how this can be applied are shown below:

- Casual, brief encounter between two friends in the street

What (field/ideational meaning)	shared experiences/ inconsequential subject matter
Who (tenor/interpersonal meaning)	roughly equal
How (mode/textual meaning)	spoken, informal

- Teacher job interview

What (field/ideational meaning)	educational (technical), questions pre-planned
Who (tenor/interpersonal meaning)	unequal, interviewers have more power
How (mode/textual meaning)	spoken, formal

Now whether such direct correspondences and relationships occur so seamlessly at the interface of context and text is highly debatable. It is not always easy to sustain such direct correspondences and more recent developments of this account, in particular Martin's 'genre' model (1986, 1992), tend to invert the virtual/actual dynamic to a more deterministic one, a point discussed in more detail on p.23.

Halliday described these various types of meanings as 'meta-functions', hence his notion of a functional model of language. Yet, while it is plausible and useful to understand how texts function in terms of representing events or ideas, indicate social meanings and relationships, and function formally as types of texts, such an understanding can skew what philosophers of language such as Wittgenstein (1953) and Austin (1962) argued to be more funda-mental and dynamic aspects of language – what they called 'language games'. Nevertheless, in the context of this book, where we are limiting our technical understanding of language to a class-room context and the mode or medium of writing in particular, it is useful at the very least to understand how Halliday's functional model has given us concepts, such as register, which have been so influential in informing current theories of genre.

For Halliday every text is unique, due to the dynamic relation-ship between context and text. From this point of view, there is not a fixed number of registers, but rather it is an unquantifiable cate-gory, so that texts are individual rather than generic. This is not to say that Halliday does not recognise genres as relatively stable tex-tual forms, but he sees them as part of the contextual variable of 'mode'. Martin on the other hand sees genre as an overriding or determining category driven by ideology and purpose, although this is an over-simplification of Martin's approach to genre. The attrac-tion of the Hallidayan model, however, is the dynamic nature of the virtual/actual interface of context and text. In other words, texts are actualised through the range of dynamic variables at play in the contexts of their production. This is a point that has major implications for the teaching of text and genre in classrooms (see Watkins 1999 for further discussion of this point).

As you will soon see, however, while the theoretical position of genre taken in this book maintains a functional orientation, it is significantly different to both the Halliday and Martin perspectives. A key difference is that texts are more than linguistic artefacts, they are strategies, games, instructions and, in general, ways of getting things done. Halliday, for example, would see the 'field' of context being realised in the 'ideational meaning' of the text through particular aspects of the grammar. It can be problematic, however, to stratify texts into levels of meaning as the relationships are reciprocal, or interrelated, rather than structural. For example, consider the following requests:

1   Sir, would you please mind stepping aside.
2   Get out of the way clown.

In 1, the grammar is working hard to express politeness in order to get the person to do what is wanted; a term of respect is used and half of the words spoken deal with politeness and only 'stepping aside' represents what is being requested. So you could say that over half has to do with the interpersonal relations and the minority deals with representational meaning. In 2, the language is largely representational (both literal and figurative), but embedded within the language and grammar are quite forceful interpersonal relations. In other words, it is very difficult to stratify the meaning of 2 into representational and interpersonal meanings. Take the use of the word 'clown' for example, it has representational and figurative meanings, as well as a strong interpersonal meaning. It is therefore difficult to stratify its meaning grammatically in any definitive sense.

In many respects, while Halliday's functional model of language attempts to account for the social forces acting on language, it does so by reducing the potential of social situations and formations to the limits of linguistic and grammatical structures. The Danish linguist Hjelmslev (1961) was concerned with the problems of stratifying language. His solution was to propose that there were many strata and at each stratum there were the variables 'form of content' and 'form of expression' operating at the same time. So, in the above example, the word 'clown' has the form or potential to be used literally or figuratively, and in the context of this sentence it has the expression of being demeaning and insulting. In summary, the question of context and its relationship with the notion of text is complex but fundamental to our understanding of how texts work. While it is useful to formalise this interface, to do so purely from a structural or linguistic perspective will inevitably be reductionist. The view of context taken in this book follows on from Hjelmslev and Halliday, in that context is seen as a virtual force acting on and generating language events in order to get things done. While language has a representational function, in that it can give us a picture of what is going on, it is more importantly a means of force or action in that it acts on people or 'affects' action or movement whether that be internal or external.

GENRE

As we discussed at the beginning of this chapter, our approach to genre primarily refers to the language processes involved in doing things with language. We therefore talk about genres in terms of processes such as describing and arguing, and we find that we use quite different structural and grammatical resources when we engage in different genres.

The term 'genre' has been around for a long time. It has been theorised from a range of perspectives, including literary studies, popular culture, linguistics, pedagogy and more recently, English /literacy education. Academic papers have been written on the multitude of ways that the term has been used over the past 2000 years or so. Genre or 'genre theory', as it has been developed in literacy education, has been articulated within two related, although fundamentally different paradigms. The Australian semiotician, Anne Freadman (1994), for example, provides us with a particularly broad notion of the term, one that certainly pushes the concept outside of the constraints or boundaries of a text. She writes that:

> First, genre is an organising concept for our cultural practices; second, any field of genres constitutes a network of contrasts according to a variety of parameters; third, genre is place occasion, function, behaviour and interactional structures: it is very rarely useful to think of it as a kind of 'text'; fourth, cultural competence involves knowing the appropriateness principle for any genre, knowing the kind of margin you have with it, being able to vary it, knowing how to shift from one to another and how many factors would be involved in any such shift.

Unfortunately, Freadman's concept of genre has had little influence in the sphere of literacy education. The major paradigm in this field comes from the school of systemic-functional linguistics, which has gained international recognition under the label of 'the Sydney School' (Johns 2002, p. 5). This approach is associated with theorists like Frances Christie, Jim Martin and Joan Rothery. It privileges language and text as a system delivered through networks and structures, over the individual, dynamic, performative aspects of language encounters. It follows a Saussurean model where langue (the language system) is the favoured object of systematic study and parole (the dynamic social activity) is considered unsuitable (Saussure 1974). Theoretically, it accounts for meaning being determined by the language system and structures of texts. Texts are produced in, and determined by, social contexts, so that it is possible to identify the determining social elements in the structure and grammar of individual texts.

As was discussed previously in this chapter, register is the term used to define the individual characteristics of a text as determined by its context. For the Sydney School, register is not seen as a particularly useful category when dealing with the relative stability of school writing. From this position, genre (as a textual category) is theorised as an abstraction or classification of real-life, everyday texts (registers). As a theory, it asks us to visualise the production of everyday texts on one level (represented as registers in Figure 1.1), so that genre must then be viewed on another level. Genres are classified according to their social purpose and identified according to the stages they move through to attain their purpose. Purpose is theorised here as a cultural category; for example, shopping would be seen as having a universal purpose, but the stages required to achieve that purpose could be conceivably different, depending on the cultural context; for example, shopping in Bangkok as opposed to Bendigo.

The model does not finish at this level. Theorists working within this paradigm claim to do more than simply provide a framework for classifying text types. They also address the issue of social equality. To do this they propose another level above genre – ideology – 'the system of coding orientations constituting a culture' (Martin 1992, p. 501).

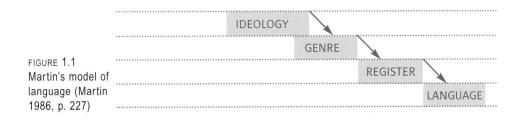

FIGURE 1.1
Martin's model of
language (Martin
1986, p. 227)

Ideology in this model is the level at which texts are contested socially. It is the level of heterogeneity, as opposed to the homogeneity of the level below which is generally out of reach to the powerless and marginalised in society. This level determines who has access to the powerful genres and is therefore crucial to the effective redistribution of power in the social order.

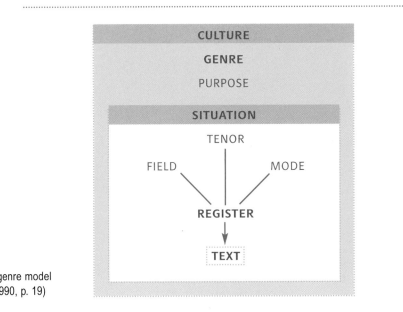

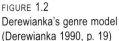
FIGURE 1.2
Derewianka's genre model
(Derewianka 1990, p. 19)

As exemplified in Figure 1.2, Martin's final level of ideology has been omitted in the model of genre proposed for teaching practice. This has resulted in a pedagogical stance that focuses on the classification of text types and their relevant structures. This failure to apply the final level of theory to practice has resulted in widespread criticism accusing 'genre' of being hostile to the cultural, cognitive and language development of students (Luke,1994; Threadgold 1992, 1993, 1994; Lee 1993; Poynton 1993). Our concern is that 'genre theory' from this perspective is reduced to a classification and structural analysis of text types, making it a reductionist theory of language-teaching based on a homogenised notion of the social, which can in turn create problems pedagogically. The pedagogical implications will be discussed in detail in Chapter 3.

THE 'GENRE AS SOCIAL PROCESS' MODEL

The alternative genre model, used less widely in Australian class-rooms, is derived from the work of Critical Linguistics in the United Kingdom in the 1970s (Fowler and Kress 1979; Kress 1979) and subsequently developed by Kress on his return to Australia in the 1980s (Kress 1982, 1985). Kress (1989) outlined a common agenda for genre theory in the context of education as follows:

- that forms of text (genres) are the result of processes of social production
- that, given the relative stability of social structures, forms of text produced in and by specific social institutions, that is, the result-ant genres, will attain a certain degree of stability and persistence over time
- that consequently, texts in their generic form are not produced *ab initio* each time by all individual (or individuals) expressing an inner meaning, but are, rather, the effects of the action of indi-vidual social agents acting both within the bounds of their social history and the constraints of particular contexts, and with a knowledge of existing generic types
- that, given the social provenance of genres, different genres 'have', convey and give access to different degrees and kinds of social power
- that genres have specifiable linguistic characteristics which are neither fully determined or largely under the control of individ-ual speakers or writers
- that knowledge of the characteristics of texts and of their social place and power can and should form a part of any curriculum, whether in one subject area, or 'across the curriculum' (p. 10).

It would be difficult for genre theorists (both systemic-functional and those working with a 'genre as social process' model) not to agree with the above propositions. Kress's approach to genre, however, differs in significant ways to the systemic-functional school. First and foremost, he refers to genres as 'forms of text' rather than text types. This is a deliberate distinction as he sees genres being formed out of the dynamics of social processes, rather than being determined by an overall social purpose. In other words, where the systemic-functionalist focus is on 'langue' or language system, Kress is more interested in what Saussure identifies as 'parole' or everyday usage. While both approaches acknowledge genres as 'social processes', the key question for Kress is 'what's going on in this text – what social dynamics are at play here?' In contrast the systemic-functional model asks 'what stages has this text been through to reach its purpose'. The former posits a complex and dynamic social situation, in relation to which texts themselves are seen as variable and complex, whereas the latter marginalises the social (ignoring it as a field of social interaction and exchange, of complex and contradictory social processes), subjecting texts to a simple classificatory operation. This difference has significant implications when it comes to developing a pedagogy that makes it possible for teachers to make the appropriate classroom interventions when teaching writing (Kress and Knapp 1992).

For the purposes of the pedagogical model proposed in this book, the former question is far more useful when teaching students to write. We have therefore increasingly favoured an approach that looks at the processes that form texts rather than structures that classify text types. Our own interest in genre has used Kress's 'social process' model as a starting point, but as stated earlier in this chapter we have also been increasingly influenced by Wittgenstein's idea of texts as 'language games'. Wittgenstein (1953) proposes meaning in terms of doing or performing. Language and meanings are always performed and exchanged by language-users within the parameters of a shared understanding of the rules and conventions of the exchanges – what he called 'language games'; for example, orders, commands, instructions, explanations, recommendations, requests, descriptions and narrations. Each can be defined in relation to the rules specifying their properties and uses. The dynamic, performative aspect of texts seems to be a far more useful model for classroom teachers than the less-flexible, structural text-type model.

The concept of 'habitus', devised by the French sociologist Bourdieu (1990), is another idea we have found useful in developing a practical working model of genre. Bourdieu sees the habitus as a set of dispositions that incline individuals to act in certain ways. These dispositions are embodied – acquired through an individual's day-to-day encounters in the world with early childhood experiences being particularly important. The habitus provides individuals with a sense of how to act and respond in the course of their daily lives. It 'orients' their actions and inclinations without strictly determining them. It gives them a 'feel for the game', a sense of what is appropriate in certain circumstances and what is not. This is how we perceive genres. Taking the above insights of Bourdieu and Wittgenstein into account, we have tried to formulate a notion of genre that recognises that they are part of a system and structured in particular ways but, more importantly, they are formed in the processes of social interactions. This idea frees us from having to dichotomise structures and processes, and enables a concept of genre that is structured while focusing on the dynamic nature of social interactions.

So, rather than working with texts as if they are structured objects, we can take a more generative approach where they are seen as an arrangement of relative constants (forms and grammatical codes) always in engagement with the potential for variation and change. This provides a basis for thinking of genres as groupings of central, relatively constant processes that can provide students with the disposition to write; a factor of course dependent on the pedagogy used to implement the approach. Genres from this perspective are not seen so much as products or text types, but as a core set of generic processes (describing, explaining, instructing, arguing and narrating). Performing these processes is based not so much on learning the stages of a variety of different text types, but on the ability to apply the relevant structural and grammatical knowledge to produce appropriate texts. Therefore, an understanding of both formal and functional aspects of grammar (or what is possible with language and how it works) is a key competency in this approach. The following is a simple diagrammatical representation of the model for the generic processes essential for school learning that is a development of the original model (Knapp 1992).

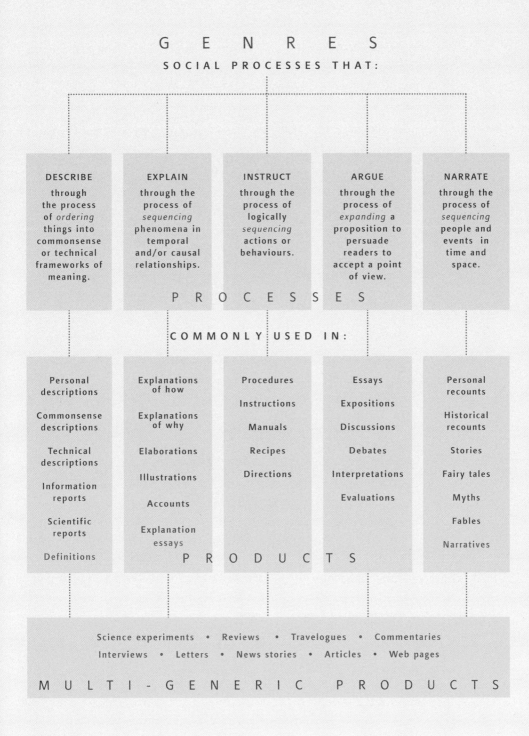

GENRES
SOCIAL PROCESSES THAT:

DESCRIBE
through the process of *ordering* things into commonsense or technical frameworks of meaning.

EXPLAIN
through the process of *sequencing* phenomena in temporal and/or causal relationships.

INSTRUCT
through the process of logically *sequencing* actions or behaviours.

ARGUE
through the process of *expanding* a proposition to persuade readers to accept a point of view.

NARRATE
through the process of *sequencing* people and events in time and space.

PROCESSES

COMMONLY USED IN:

Personal descriptions	Explanations of how	Procedures	Essays	Personal recounts
Commonsense descriptions	Explanations of why	Instructions	Expositions	Historical recounts
Technical descriptions	Elaborations	Manuals	Discussions	Stories
Information reports	Illustrations	Recipes	Debates	Fairy tales
Scientific reports	Accounts	Directions	Interpretations	Myths
Definitions	Explanation essays		Evaluations	Fables
				Narratives

PRODUCTS

Science experiments • Reviews • Travelogues • Commentaries
Interviews • Letters • News stories • Articles • Web pages

MULTI-GENERIC PRODUCTS

FIGURE 1.3
Based on Knapp's genre model (Knapp 1992, p. 13)

It is important to note that we are not being pedantic distinguishing between processes and products. It has been our experience, from a teaching/learning perspective, that the differences can be important for the following reasons:

1 Teaching genres as processes, rather than products, enables them to be applicable to all text types written by students from infants to senior secondary. That is, the generic features (structure and grammar) of the genre of describing, for example, remain consistent for all writers, from the experiential descriptions of early writers, to the scientific descriptions of senior secondary students. This enables a developmental approach to teaching that allows writers to build on and develop from what they already know about each of the genres.

2 Through teaching aspects of genres such as structure and grammar, writers will realise the generic purpose of their texts (rather than learning to reproduce 'rule-governed' formats). This enables the teaching of grammar to be a basic part of teaching programs for early writers and onwards. In other words, this shift from 'genre as product' to 'genre as process' helps avoid the criticism that teaching genres simply reduces writing texts to replicating formulas.

3 While text types can be relatively simple and straight forward in primary school, in secondary school, students are often expected to produce texts that contain more than one genre. For example, what do we call a text that first describes something, then explains how it works and finally argues for its use? An approach that sees genres as processes has no problem with multi-generic texts such as these. From this point of view it doesn't matter what label we give a text, but rather that we know what the text is doing. And more than this, that we can teach students the generic and grammatical resources required to produce both simple and complex texts.

The types of genres in contemporary society are expanding and changing. This is due, in part, to the proliferation of information technologies. Considerable emphasis has been placed on students developing competencies in reading and constructing multi-modal texts. Schools, however, need to start by teaching students the basic written genres that have been developed to deal with the exchange of information and knowledge. Competence at this level will enable students to explore the possibilities to establish a foundation for flexibility and creativity beyond the limits of written language and application within education and training.

TEXT

Language is always produced, exchanged or received as text; that is, language as a system of communication is organised as cohesive units we call texts. A text is any completed act of communication such as a greeting between friends in the street, a television advertisement, a novel, or a film and so on. As far as speech and writing are concerned, a text stands alone as an act of communication.

Different types of texts have distinctive characteristics, depending on what they are made to do. A piece of poetry, for instance, is immediately and characteristically different from a scientific description because each is doing a vastly different thing with language.

Texts can be classified and organised in a multitude of ways: everyday, formal, entertaining and informational. Traditionally, different types of texts have been identified according to established conventions: Shakespeare and Dickens are 'literary', a scientific procedure and a computer manual are 'factual', and *The Simpsons* and the *7.30 Report* are 'media' texts. How, then, do we classify a text such as Sally Morgan's autobiography, *My Place*? In the first instance it is literary in that it uses language in a way that moves or evokes in readers reflective and emotional responses. It is also factual: it is a recount of her life and puts forward powerful arguments for a change in social perceptions and understanding. Finally, it has become widely read and influential through the print media.

In the light of these problems and contradictions, however, teachers require ways of thinking about the characteristics of texts more than before. The following classifications are therefore useful as one way of thinking, and by no means absolute.

LITERARY TEXTS

For the purposes of teaching English, literary texts might include the broad range of texts that reflect and interpret individual and social life, whether real or imaginary. Literary texts can deal with everyday experience in a way that lifts readers beyond the everyday.

Literary texts use language in a way that moves it beyond the concrete representational and functional modes of language. Literary texts often use language to create images in readers' minds; the language enables readers to engage with the text and incorporate their own meanings and understandings with those of the writer. Literary texts make greater use of figural language (metaphor, rhythm, repetition) and poetics (language for the sake of language) than do everyday texts. Literary texts include novels, epics, poems, dramas and sagas.

FACTUAL TEXTS

Factual texts, from the point of view of schooling, include those texts that have the primary aim of communicating knowledge as it has been educationally defined, classified and constructed. Factual texts deal with the exchange of knowledge (learning) in all of the learning areas. In the everyday sense they include all of the texts that we use from day to day to 'get things done'. Many factual texts such as technical descriptions, explanations and procedures tend to be driven by purpose and seek to be efficient and effective in their transmission. Other factual texts, such as essays, reviews and arguments, are more rhetorical and take time to position and persuade readers.

MEDIA TEXTS

This classification of texts is problematical for a range of reasons, not least of which is that the modalities are changing and developing literally before our eyes. For example, much is made of the impact on spelling and syntax of SMS and emails. Such discussions are outside the scope of this book; however, as discussed earlier in this chapter, one of the dynamic variables of any concept of text is the potential for users to make it their own. In light of this, it is important that the forms and modalities of media texts impact on the literacy experiences of all students. From this perspective we need to recognise that media texts are any texts (whether literary or factual) that are used in channels of mass communication such as print, broadcasting, cable, film and video.

Depending on the media, these texts can use different modes of communication: writing, speech, pictures or sound or all of these. The shape of media texts is determined to some extent by the technology employed by the particular media. An understanding of such texts would necessarily imply an understanding of the technologies and modes of production of the respective media.

In the learning area of English, students are expected to gain a competent understanding of how English works in all of the above categories of texts. For example, the type of language deployed to write a poem will be vastly different from that required for a set of instructions. English, in its more functional modes, will be able to be effectively taught in the context of the other learning areas. In its more figural or literary modes, however, it will have to be taught as English. In order to give students a technical understanding of how texts work, teachers will need to use a technical language for the task. Without such a 'language about language', the acquisition of this knowledge would be quite difficult in many cases and almost impossible in others.

GRAMMAR

One of the cornerstones of this approach to genre, text and grammar is the relationship generated between genre and grammar. While systemic-functional grammar forges a relationship between context and grammar, as we have seen, such a relationship is often problematic. In many respects the gap between context and grammar is simply too wide, often resulting in deterministic relationships. The genre and grammar-based approach creates a closer congruity as the concept of genre is not deterministic or derivative, but relies upon the relationship between social purpose and available grammatical resources.

We need to explain this further before proceeding with a broader explanation of the relationship between genres and their relevant grammars. In the first instance, it is difficult to develop a pedagogic grammar based on the three strata of interpretation as proposed by Halliday. As was discussed earlier in this chapter, such a stratification is often difficult to maintain across the diversity of language events we are calling texts. In most respects, language is a stable system of possibilities. Context, as we have described it above, is a virtual or potential framework for the production of texts. Our purpose here is to identify the relationships between the virtual nature of context and actual texts, which is where the notion of genre is fundamental. Without genre, grammar is too abstract to be effectively teachable. Grammar remains simply a set of rules for correctness or appropriateness. This is one of the key reasons that progressivism rejected grammar, as it was seen as a set of rules for social conformity.

Grammar is one of our key literacy technologies. Without a knowledge of grammar the process of becoming literate becomes hazardous. The question of grammar and how it should be taught becomes one of the key focus points for all that follows in this book. Indeed, the great strength of our process-based approach to genre and grammar is the connections emphasised between genre and grammar. Pedagogically, grammar only becomes meaningful when it is linked to the purpose and function of texts.

WHAT IS GRAMMAR?

There are many different grammars developed for different purposes. Traditional-type grammars were developed to describe and analyse the way that words are put together within sentences. These traditional or syntactical-type grammars use different types of terminologies, depending on whether a word is being classified as a type of word − for example, a noun, an adjective, an adverb and so on − or whether it is described by its function or what it is doing; for example, subject, object, predicate and so on.

In this book we are more concerned with a way of using grammar to describe how particular texts are put together. In other words, as well as describing what is going on within sentences, we are also concerned with how language is used at the levels of text and genre. Grammar from this point of view is a name for the resources available to users of a language system for producing texts. A knowledge of grammar by a speaker or writer shifts language use from the implicit and unconscious to a conscious manipulation of language and choice of appropriate texts.

From this point of view a genre-based grammar focuses on the manner through which different language processes or genres in writing are coded in distinct and recognisable ways.

It first considers how a text is structured and organised due to the characteristics of particular genres in relation to purpose, audience, message and structure. It then considers how all parts of the text − such as sentences, tense, reference, cohesion and so on − are structured, organised and coded, so as to make the text effective as written communication and, in particular, how all the parts are used to serve the purposes of the language users.

Finally, a genre-based grammar will deal with the syntactical aspects of grammar or how the language is organised within sentences; for example, the appropriate use of prepositions, plurals, articles, agreement and so on.

A knowledge of grammar in this sense is not just concerned with rules for what can and can't be done with the organisation and use of words in English sentences, but also with the way written English functions to communicate experiences and knowledge of the world. In addition, narrative genres often deliberately break the rules of grammar and punctuation for literary effect.

The genre and grammar model of language we are describing requires us to become aware of the forms that language takes in the social contexts in which texts are commonly used. It requires us to look at the structures and grammatical features that make up these forms, and to look at the way that language serves the intentions of those who use and produce it, as well as the effects it has for audiences. This perspective also locates language as a social practice that makes us active participants in the organisation and exchange of meaning. To fully participate in any social activity for making meaning, we need to have at our disposal the technical resources for using language across the wide range of social situations that make up our everyday lives. Grammar therefore needs to deal with language from three perspectives: the generic, the textual and the syntactical. This is a far broader view of grammar than has traditionally been the case. Traditional grammar was mainly concerned with syntax, or how words are correctly ordered within a sentence. We, on the other hand, consider how genres themselves make particular demands on the grammatical choices we have when producing a text. Why, for instance, is it that when we describe we use particular sentence types, tense and structures that are recognisably different to when we use the genre of instructing or arguing?

From a technical point of view, grammatical terms fall into two broad categories: formal and functional. The formal categories give us a way of classifying the bits and pieces that constitute sentences and texts. The functional categories on the other hand help us understand what the bits and pieces are doing. For example, terms like noun, adverb and adjective are formal categories because they formally classify types of words: a noun is the name of a thing, an adverb is a word that modifies the meaning of a verb or adjective and so on. Words like subject, object and predicate, on the other hand, are terms that tell us how nouns, adverbs and adjectives are being used in a sentence. In order to have a useful technical description for what is happening with language we need to have a terminology that describes both form and function.

FORMAL ASPECTS OF GRAMMAR

Understanding the formal aspects of grammar means giving consideration to how the English language is put together. As a language system, there are particular arrangements and forms that all users are required to follow. Things like the arrangement of the subject, verb and object in English sentences may seem 'natural' to native users, but can be quite unnatural to users of other languages as not all languages are organised in terms of SVO (subject, verb, object). Other things, such as subject/verb agreement and tense are formal aspects of grammar; they have to do with the formal characteristics of the English language. Other formal aspects of grammar can be difficult to non–English-speaking background students. In English we mark tense by changing the form of the verb and using appropriate auxiliaries. Other languages do not change the form of the verb to mark tense. In English we cannot begin a statement with a verb, however, in other languages it may be normal to do so.

Broadly speaking, however, the formal categories of grammar are the eight parts of speech identified by Thrax in 100 BC. These are noun, pronoun, verb, adverb, adjective, preposition, conjunction and interjection (later in English grammars the article became a part of speech). While these classes of words were developed to define the language demands of ancient Greek and Latin, English has inherited them onwards from the fourteenth century, even though English is quite hybridised in many respects. These formal categories, however, do provide us with a useful and highly recognisable classification system for types of words.

These formal aspects of language, often referred to as 'traditional grammar', formed a significant part of the English curriculum taught in schools up until the past 20 or so years, and have only recently been reintroduced into English syllabus documents. Texts also have formal characteristics; some texts such as recounts and explanations have a basic form of sequencing units of information. Other texts, such as descriptions and reports, formally order things into ways of knowing them.

FUNCTIONAL ASPECTS OF GRAMMAR

Functional aspects of grammar are concerned with what the language is doing, or better, being made to do. While it is essential for us as users of the language system to know the limitations and possibilities of the system itself, it is also important to be aware of the choices available to get things done. Although we tend to think of the rules of grammar as being firmly fixed, language is in fact a very pliable system that responds subtly to the constantly changing demands made on it by its users. The more we know about what the language is doing, the greater chance we will have to make it work for us as speakers and writers.

Although it may seem confusing at first to have parallel sets of terminologies for describing language, in many respects it is unavoidable because different classes of words can function differently according to how we use them; for example, nouns can be the subject and object of a sentence:

article	noun	verb	article	noun	formal
The	boy	hit	the	ball.	
subject		verb	object		functional

The functional terminology tells us what we can and cannot do with an English sentence. Take the following very simple sentence as an example in English we cannot write:

The ball	the boy	hit.
object	subject	verb

or

Hit	the ball	the boy.
verb	object	subject

FIGURAL ASPECTS OF GRAMMAR

Finally, the figural aspects of grammar look at how language communicates beyond the concrete representational level. In other words, language can represent things/actions/events in concrete terms, as in the above example, where there is a boy involved in the act of hitting a ball. Often, however, we use words and language to represent more than the concrete. The figural, therefore, is a way of talking about language when it moves beyond the concrete. It looks at how language can be used to create images to carry additional meanings. Figures of speech such as metaphor, for example, achieve their effect by using a concrete representation of something else to create a semantic effect beyond the original meaning, such as in the following:

> The boy smashed the ball over the bowler's head.

The verb to smash is here being used in a figural sense; it is telling us a lot more than simply 'hitting'. Smashing gives us a picture of the shot; the choice of this verb provides us with a vivid image, as well as telling us what happened. Where the verb *to hit* is multipurpose, in that it represents a generalised act across a range of circumstances, the verb *to smash* gives us a picture of the way the ball was hit, and the attitude of the person reporting on the shot. The use of the figural is very important in literary and media texts. Figural language enables writers to trigger images with readers that relay their meaning more intensely and efficiently than relying on strictly concrete language. For example:

> At the end of the show the crowd quickly left the theatre, filling the surrounding streets.

compared to

> At the end of the show the crowd spilled into the street.

Metaphor is a constant factor in all language use. When we say 'The library opens at 9 a.m.', we treat 'library' as though it could act of its own volition. When we say 'The milk came to the boil', we use a form that is metaphorical (compare 'The child came to the door'). Metaphor, therefore, operates at all levels of language; from mundane to the literary, and everywhere in between.

CONNECTING GENRE, TEXT AND GRAMMAR

As we have seen, genre, text and grammar are the three basic categories for the model of language proposed here. The key to its usefulness, however, is that it is able to make explicit connections between:

- genre, the social context and relations in which texts are produced
- text, the language processes we use to construct products
- grammar, the choices and limitations language-users have when putting words together in texts.

In chapters 4 to 8 we examine each of the five genres of school writing, detailing the grammar generic to each and examples of various texts that writers can produce when using these technologies within the classroom context. Prior to this, in Chapter 2 we provide a glossary of grammatical terms and in Chapter 3 we outline the pedagogic approach we favour in teaching students to make connections between genre, text and grammar in their writing.

A GENRE-BASED GRAMMAR

As was discussed in Chapter 1, grammar is an overwhelmingly vexed issue – one that raises polemical and at times irrational and uninformed argument. In the context of schooling and teaching writing in New South Wales, Australia, in the 1990s, the 'functional vs traditional' grammar argument exemplified an aspect of the futility of the past 200 years of debate on the value of teaching grammar. Our position, however, has the aim of showing how debates like 'new vs old' and 'traditional vs functional' are unproductive as all grammars are necessarily both formal and functional. It would therefore follow that to dichotomise such fundamental elements is of little use in the development of an approach to grammar primarily concerned with its role in the production of texts in the context of the school curriculum.

A problem with many traditional grammars is that they can easily be used in classrooms as manuals for 'correctness' in that they tend to standardise dialect and what the Russian language theorist Bakhtin (1952) calls 'accent' – individual inflections of language.

The prescriptiveness of grammar has presented a problem for educators resulting in it almost disappearing from mainstream education towards the latter part of last century. Grammar, from this perspective, has been demonised, with it being blamed rather than the way it has been used pedagogically. In this chapter we will propose that grammar in itself is a productive potentiality, a technology useful in its role of helping make the processes of writing conscious for students.

By and large, grammar first needs to be taught and used primarily in the context of reading and writing. Grammar taught out of context has the potential to be reduced to rules and standardised usage. However, the relationship of context to grammar, as discussed in the previous chapter, is often represented as a reductionist model where grammar attempts to account for context.

Up until relatively recently, grammar was mainly concerned with describing the formal and notional characteristics of language. Since the development of structural linguistics, in particular the work of Chomsky (1965), linguists have been broadening grammatical terminology to describe both the formal and functional characteristics of language. In particular, functional linguists, such as Halliday, have required a grammar to describe the way that speech is used in everyday contexts, requiring them to focus on categories that help describe elements such as 'function', 'use' and 'purpose', rather than the formal 'parts of speech'. The problem with modern grammars from a point of view of teaching writing, however, is that they have been primarily developed for describing 'speech in use' and therefore are not directly transferable as a technology for teaching students to use writing for the variety of uses required in schooling. This is acknowledged by Martin and Rothery (1993, p. 145), who write that functional grammar is primarily 'for linguists and their apprentices not for teachers and their students in schools'.

Our use of grammar in this book is framed in the context of education rather than linguistics. The first premise is that there is something to be taught about writing. From this it follows that grammar must be part of the equation, simply from the point of view of having a metalanguage for talking about writing. No grammars can be entirely formal or entirely functional, and to construe grammars in such oppositional terms is less than productive. From one point of view there is a need to see grammar as a technology for classifying and describing what people are able to do with language: both as speech and writing; how and why they do it; and to utilise this technology in writing themselves. From another point of view, grammar needs to be taught as a potential and generative function within language, and in so doing to help students become conscious of the grammar they already use in their own writing.

What should be clear at this point is that we are not proposing that grammar should be taught as a thing in itself. Grammar should not be seen as a stand-alone set of rules and definitions, but rather as a 'force of expression' within genre. In other words, when we use the genre of describing we use a particular set of language resources, or grammar, that is different in many key respects to what we use when we use the genre of instructing, which is different to when we are using the genre of arguing and so on. On the one hand, grammar is a metalanguage that we can share so that as teachers and learners of writing we can use grammar to systematically describe and explain how language is being used for particular purposes. For example, it is important when we are discussing what is going on in a sentence that we understand the difference between an 'adverb' and an 'adverbial'; or that we can explain to students why one sentence works better than another. Grammar therefore provides us with the technical understanding of language to then effectively and efficiently teach it to students.

Our approach to grammar in this book is therefore fundamentally pedagogical. In the following chapters, where each of the genres is systematically outlined, the grammar of each genre is described and exemplified. In addition, we describe how the relevant grammar can be taught in the context of the genre and finally we demonstrate how we can use our knowledge of the generic and grammatical features to diagnostically assess student writing and how to address problems and allow students to improve their writing.

This chapter therefore is a resource where grammatical terms are listed alphabetically to assist ease of reference. It is worth noting that the definitions and examples that we provide here are given in the context of the pedagogical chapters that are to follow. We have deliberately used traditional terminology, even though our definitions may have more of a functional emphasis than most so-called traditional grammars. Finally, a note about punctuation – although grammar and punctuation are often treated as separate issues, from a pedagogical perspective it is important to look at the relationship of each to effective writing. The function of punctuation in sentence structure, for example, is critical. We use punctuation to define the boundaries of our sentences and it is fundamental that students be taught the function of punctuation when being taught the structural aspects of sentence construction and syntax. For this reason we have included definitions and examples of punctuation in the following glossary.

ADJECTIVE

Adjectives are describing words that tend to be used in two ways: before a noun attributively as a pre-modifier, and after a verb predicatively as a complement to the subject or object of a clause.

An <u>unruly</u> playground often means an *unhappy* school.	Pre-modifiers
The playground appears *unruly*.	Post-modifier predicating the subject
Parents find the playground *unruly*.	Post-modifier predicating the object

When there is more than one adjective before a noun there is a conventional order; that is, moving from the general to the specific, such as:

the slow, green, river steamer **not** the green, slow, river steamer

ADJECTIVAL CLAUSE

See Clauses.

ADJECTIVAL PHRASE

An adjectival phrase is a group of words introduced by a preposition that gives additional information about a noun.

The reason *for these strict playground rules* is to maintain order.

ADVERB

Adverbs are words that modify or add information to the meaning of verbs by specifying the time or place of an action, or the manner in which it was performed. These types of adverbs often end in 'ly'.

The girl ran *quickly* across the road. He *studiously* read the required reading matter.

Adverbs can also modify adjectives and other adverbs, as in adverbs of degree such as *very, really, almost, quite.*

ADVERBIAL

The term adverbial is a functional category and does not necessarily refer to adverbs although it can. Adverbials (A) are often optional elements in sentences. They can be one word or a group of words that locate the time, place or manner in which the action (the verb) was performed. They can be identified by asking how, where, when or in what way something happened. There can be any number of adverbials in a sentence and their position is not fixed. For example:

On Saturdays	Pauline	often	jogs	briskly	around the park	for an hour.
adverbial [time]	subject	adverb	verb	adverb	adverbial [place]	adverbial [time]

Often for an hour	on Saturdays	Pauline	jogs	briskly	around the park.
adverbial [time]	adverbial [time]	subject	verb	adverb	adverbial [place]

ADVERBIAL CLAUSE

See Clauses.

ADVERBIAL PHRASE

An adverbial phrase is a group of words beginning with a preposition. It provides additional information about the time, place or manner of whatever is going on in a clause.

The local park is mostly used *after school each day*.
In the mornings traffic is at its worst.

AGREEMENT

Verbs change their form to agree with their subjects. With simple verbs, differences in the verb form only occur in the present tense and only when using third-person singular. It is shown by adding 's'. For example:

I (or you, we or they) often *cross* at the lights.
She (he or it) often *crosses* at the lights.
The children (or they) often *cross* at the lights.

In verb groups, it is the first element that must agree with the subject. When the first element is an auxiliary verb, as in the verbs 'to be', 'to have' or 'to do', the form of the auxiliary changes for first person singular and plural as well as third person singular and plural. For example:

I *am* crossing the road.	First person singular
We *are* crossing the road.	First person plural
She *is* crossing the road.	Third person singular
They *are* crossing the road.	Third person plural

Note, if the verb group has a modal auxiliary then the auxiliary does not change its form to mark agreement. For example, if the auxiliary is the verb 'to have' the modal 'may' does not change:

She **has** used the pedestrian crossing.	Third person singular
They *have* used the pedestrian crossing.	Third person plural
She *may* **have** used the pedestrian crossing.	Third person singular
They *may* have used the pedestrian crossing.	Third person plural

APOSTROPHES

Apostrophes are primarily used in punctuation to indicate:

1 possession or attributes

the *school's* playground equipment	Possession
the *school's* location	Attribute

2 contraction or omission of a letter from a word – I'll (I will), can't (cannot).

We'll	We will
can't	cannot
won't	will not

The rule for possession in the case of most singular nouns is to place an *apostrophe* and *s* after the word. The rule for possession in the case of most plural nouns is to place an apostrophe only after the word (*most schools' playgrounds*). Plural nouns that do not end in *s* take an *apostrophe and s* after the word (*the children's books*). The apostrophe is **not** needed to indicate possession with the pronouns *hers, its, theirs* and *yours* as they are already possessive.

ARTICLES

There are two types of articles: definite *(the)* and indefinite *(a/an)*. Articles function to tell us that a noun or noun group is about to follow. Definite articles tell us that the noun is referring to a specific thing, indefinite articles refer to classes of things. Not all languages use articles and so students from some language backgrounds other than English may omit them from their spoken and written English.

The park is situated near *the* shopping centre.	Definite
A truck was seen running *a* red light.	Indefinite

When reference is made to people or things as generic classes, either the definite or indefinite article can be used for the singular and no article should be used for the plural.

The elephant is an animal.

An elephant is an animal.

Elephants are animals.

See Determiners.

BRACKETS

Brackets or parentheses are used to enclose material that provides additional information or comment within an otherwise complete sentence (round brackets are normally used for this function). Square brackets are used to enclose material that was not written by the author of the sentence.

CAPITAL LETTERS

Capital letters are used at the beginning of sentences, for proper nouns (the names of people and places, months of year, days of the week) and for titles (Mr, Mrs, Doctor, Lord Mayor).

CLAUSES

The clause is the basic grammatical unit in a sentence. A main clause usually consists of a subject (the thing being identified for comment) and a predicate (the comment about the subject). The predicate in a main clause always contains a finite verb. A main clause is a clause that can stand alone as a complete sentence. The number of clauses and the relationship between them in a sentence is the basis for distinguishing types of sentences (see simple, compound and complex sentences). If a sentence has two main clauses that are joined with an additive conjunction they are said to be in a coordinating relationship. If a sentence has a main clause and one or more additional clauses that are dependent on the main clause for their meaning then they are said to be in a subordinating relationship.

Clauses that are not main clauses do not necessarily need a finite verb. For example, non-finite and verbless clauses provide additional information to the meaning of a sentence without being located in time with a finite verb.

Through reducing the speed limit schools will become safer environments.	Non-finite dependent clause
Because of the reduction of the speed limit schools will become safer environments.	Verbless dependent clause

ADJECTIVAL CLAUSE

A clause that gives additional information about a noun or noun group is known as an adjectival or relative clause, and is said to be 'embedded' as the information it provides is embedded or located within the subject or object of another clause. They generally begin with a relative pronoun such as who, which or that.

Rules *that are carefully monitored* help to make the playground a safe environment.	Subject
All playgrounds need rules *that people should obey*.	Object

ADVERBIAL CLAUSE

An adverbial clause is a subordinate or dependent clause that provides optional information about time, place, condition, concession, reason, purpose and result *to what is happening in the main clause*.

When children first arrive at school they need to know what to do.	Time
Although there are other parks nearby there are none close to the shopping centre.	Concession
New traffic lights have been installed near the school *because of the heavy traffic flow*.	Reason

NOMINAL CLAUSE

A nominal clause is a clause that acts as the subject or object of another clause. Nominal clauses are not considered to be embedded because the information they provide has a dependent relationship with the information in the clause of which they are a part.

The Council's decision to create a car park is not in the interests of children.	Subject position
The children in the local area believe *that the Council should reconsider its decision*.	Object position

VERBLESS CLAUSE

A verbless clause is a clause where the subject and verb is ellipted/ understood or nominalised.

Whether diesel or petrol vehicles produce unacceptable levels of pollution.	Subject/verb (they are) ellipted
In the interests of the local children, the council should reconsider its decision.	Subject/verb nominalised

It is considered a clause because it is dealing with a separate piece of information in relation to the main clause. For example, in the sentence, *In the interests of the local children,* the council should reconsider its decision, there are two separate pieces of information: the main clause – the council should reconsider its decision; and a dependent clause that deals with issues that *interest* local children. In this clause, however, the verb has been nominalised resulting in a verbless clause. Verbless clauses are different from adverbial phrases. The latter provide some information to do with the time, place or manner in which something happens within an existing clause. Verbless clauses, on the other hand, provide a separate piece of information outside of an existing clause.

COHESION

Grammatically, cohesion refers to the devices available to help link information in writing and help the text flow and hold together. The three key devices are ellipsis, conjunctions and pronouns.

COLONS

Colons are used to introduce something. They are normally used to signal the following:

* a list
  The reasons for keeping the park are: the environment, recreation and appearance.

- an example (or examples)
  There are many types of vehicles: cars, buses, trucks and motorcycles.

- an explanation
  One result is inevitable: someone will eventually be injured.

- a subtitle
  Traffic and Pollution: The Awful Bedfellows.

COMMAS

Commas are used within sentences to separate information into readable units and guide the reader as to the relationship between phrases and items in a series (serious, premeditated and cold-blooded action). Commas act like markers to help the reader voice the meaning of long sentences. For example, when sentences begin with a subordinate clause or phrase, commas indicate to the reader where the main clause begins.

COMPLEMENT

The complement is a functional category used when describing the constituent elements of a simple sentence. As the name implies, it complements the meaning of either the subject or object of a main clause. For example,

| The playground became *a civilised environment*. | Complementing the subject |
| Most people considered the playground *a safer place*. | Complementing the object |

CONJUNCTS

Conjuncts are adverbials that connect clauses or sentences logically. They are mainly adverbs such as *therefore, perhaps, however, consequently* or prepositional phrases such as: *as a result of, on the other hand, as a consequence of* and so on. (See Connectives.)

CONJUNCTIONS

A conjunction is a class of words that either coordinates words or clauses of equal status such as:

The playground rules were strict **but** fair.
The rules for the playground were proposed by the staff **and** discussed at the school council.

or, subordinates a clause to its superordinate clause, which can either be a main clause or another subordinate clause. For example,

Because the playground rules were fair, the students were cooperative.
The rules worked best *when* teachers supervised the playground.

(See Connectives.)

CONNECTIVES

Connective is a functional term for words like conjuncts and conjunctions that join linguistic units such as sentences, clauses, phrases and words in logical relationships of time, cause and effect, comparison or addition. Connectives relate people, things and ideas to one another, and help to show the logic of the information. The logical relationships can be grouped thus:

first, second, third, etc., when, now, meanwhile, finally, next, lastly afterward, soon, then, here, previously, before, until, till, while, whenever	Temporal
as, because, for, since, so, consequently, hence, therefore, thus, yet, still, however, though, nevertheless, hence	Causal
elsewhere, rather, instead, also, alternatively, in other respects, on the other hand	Comparative
and, or, nor, also, furthermore, additionally, besides, likewise, similarly, alternatively whereas, also, while, as well as	Additive
and, nor, for, yet, but, or, so	Coordinating

DETERMINERS

A determiner is a functional category for words that determine or limit a noun or noun group to be either definite (this, the, our) or indefinite (a, some, much). Determiners can be articles, pronouns, or adjectives and can be divided into three groups:

- Central determiners
  - articles:
    a cricketer (indefinite)
    the white ball (definite)

  - demonstratives:
    this aircraft, those thunderstorms

  - possessives:
    my life, your seatbelt

  - quantifiers:
    each delivery, every moment, any time

- Post-determiners (used after central determiners)
  - numbers or numeratives:
    the first five balls, my first truck

  - quantifiers:
    our last dance, the many occasions

- Pre-determiners (used before central determiners)
  - quantifiers:
    all the time, both the houses, half the area

  - multipliers:
    double the money, twice the size, three times the height

  - exclamations:
    what a good catch, such a brilliant stroke

ELLIPSIS

Ellipsis is the omission of a word or structural part of a sentence or clause. The ellipted element is understood by the reader from the textual context. Grammatical ellipsis enables writers to achieve economy by avoiding having to repeat lexical and structural elements that can be retrieved or understood by the reader by what has preceded or what follows the ellipted element. For example,

Your car is much quieter than mine (my car is).
Year 4 boys did not want to play as much as the Year 6s (boys did).

EMBEDDING

Embedding is a functional term used to describe ways of attaching additional information to the subject or object of clauses. As can be seen in the examples of post-modification in noun groups, embedding can take the form of phrases or clauses. For example,

A blanket *made of wool* is best for . warmth.	Adjectival clause modifying the subject
Always take a blanket *preferably made of wool*.	Adjectival clause modifying the object
A blanket *with a high wool content* is best for warmth.	Adjectival phrase modifying the subject
Always take a blanket *with a high wool content*.	Adjectival phrase modifying the object

Embedded clauses and phrases generally indicate an ability to condense and order information in a text. As such, they represent a higher order of subordination in sentence structure. In formal terms, most embedded clauses are adjectival or relative clauses. Another feature of embedded clauses is that the clause is part of the structure of another clause and therefore does not have a coordinating or subordinating relationship with the main clause. For example, in the following sentence there is a main clause (**in bold**) that has an embedded adjectival clause post-modifying the object (*italics*), followed by a dependent clause (underlined).

Remember not to disturb any flora or fauna *that you may see* as they are protected by law.

The following provides a diagrammatical representation:

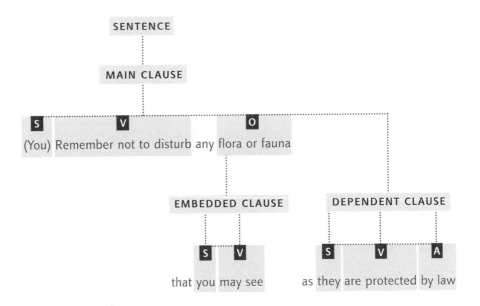

Embedded clauses are also a feature of better literary writing. In the following sentence, an adjectival clause (**in bold**) post-modifies the noun group that is the subject of the main clause (<u>underlined</u>). You will note that this type of embedding is an effective technique in focusing on the image for impact.

<u>The empty eye-sockets</u> **that were abandoned warehouse windows** glared eerily down at me from their high vantage point.

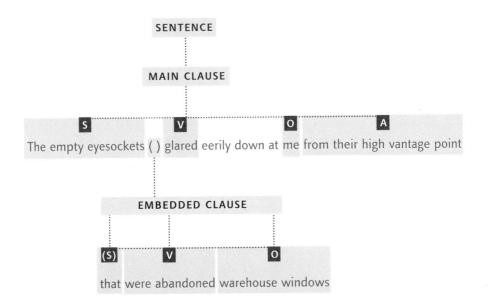

Note that the above sentence is essentially a simple sentence as the embedded adjectival clause is not in a coordinating or subordinating relationship with the main clause.

In order to identify an embedded clause as opposed to a subordinate clause use the following test. An embedded clause will have a dependent relationship with either the subject or object of another clause rather than the clause itself.

EXCLAMATION MARK

The exclamation mark is most often used in written dialogue and reported speech to emphasise interactive force in the words. Most commonly it is used in the following:

Hi! Good evening! G'day!	Greetings
Get out of the way!	Commands
Hear, hear!	Interjections
What a shot!	Exclamatives

FIGURATIVE LANGUAGE OR FIGURES OF SPEECH

These refer to the techniques of language that help construct associated images in the mind of the reader or create a deliberate literary effect.

ALLITERATION

Alliteration is the figurative technique of repeating the same sound, usually the initial consonant of a word, for narrative, literary or rhetorical effect. For example,

The problem of poisonous pollution is politically damaging.

CLICHÉ

Cliché is generally a pejorative term for the use of a word or phrase, or a figure of speech like a simile or metaphor, that has lost its effect through overuse. For example,

thick as a brick, seriously speaking, he fought like a demon, she was a jewel

HYPERBOLE

A rhetorical term used to describe over-statement or exaggeration. It is not generally meant to be taken literally. For example,

a thousand apologies, as old as the hills

METAPHOR

A metaphor is a figure of speech where one thing is named as another. The effect is to draw an association, comparison or resemblance in the mind of the reader that enhances the imagery being created by the writer. For example,

The playground was a cauldron of activity.

METONYMY

A figure of speech similar to metaphor but designates something by the name of something associated with it. For example,

the bottle for alcoholic drink	He took to the bottle after the war.
the crown for the monarchy	He was a citizen of the crown.
the stage for the theatre	She followed a life on the stage.

RHETORICAL QUESTION

A question that does not expect an answer, but rather creates the rhetorical effect of signalling to the reader that the answer is given and therefore unarguable. For example,

Where do we go from here?
What is the point of going on?

SIMILE

A simile is a figure of speech that makes a comparison between one thing and another, usually in a phrase beginning with, *like* or *as*. The two things being compared must be different, and the quality being compared must be familiar to the reader in one of the things. The image created is set alongside the original statement, not replacing or subsuming it as a metaphor would.

The flow of traffic moves *like a snake*.
The pollution is *as thick as soup*.

SYNECDOCHE

Synecdoche is a figure of speech where the part is used to represent the whole or where the whole is used to represent the part. For example,

All hands on deck.   where hands represent the sailor

Australia has beaten   where the whole country represents the team
England at Lords.

FULL STOP

Full stops are used to mark the end of sentences. Full stops may also be used to indicate abbreviations, although this convention is variable in its usage and the current trend is to omit full stops when abbreviating upper-case and people's initials.

MODALITY

The term 'modality' describes a range of grammatical resources used to express probability or obligation. Generally, obligation is used in speech, especially when wanting to get things done such as 'You should keep your room tidy'. In writing, modality of probability is used to indicate the degree or qualification of a writer's position in relation to absolute truth or fact, in order to manipulate a reader's perspective such as 'It *may* be necessary to punish those who disobey rules'. Modality is expressed through various grammatical devices:

can, should, will, might	Modal auxiliaries
possible (indicating probability, usuality, presumption, inclination, time, degree, intensity)	Modal adverbs
possibility	Modal nouns
possible	Modal adjectives

MODAL ADVERBS

Modal adverbs express the writer's judgement regarding the 'truth' of a proposition. They typically appear just before or after the finite element. They can, however, appear at the start of the proposition. The following list of modal adverbs classifies them according to their typical use.

certainly, surely, probably, perhaps, maybe, possibly, definitely, positively	Probability/ obligation
always, often, usually, regularly, typically, occasionally, seldom, rarely, ever, never, once	Usuality
evidently, apparently, presumably, clearly, no doubt, obviously, of course, personally, honestly	Presumption
gladly, willingly, readily	Inclination
yet, still, already, once, soon, just	Time
quite, almost, nearly, totally, entirely, utterly, completely, literally, absolutely, scarcely, hardly, on the whole, provisionally	Degree
just, simply, ever, only, really, actually, seriously	Intensity

RHETORICAL FUNCTION OF MODALITY

Writing has two important functions: one is representational in that it is telling the reader about something; the other is rhetorical in that it is positioning the reader to accept the truth or importance of what is being said. Modality is an important resource in the latter function. Writers often use adjectives and nouns in this way as an effective persuasive device. For example,

It is *necessary* to take a first aid kit.	adjective

This is a different use of the adjective 'necessary' to the following, where is used to describe a piece of equipment.

A first aid kit is a necessary item to take.

NOMINALISATION

Nominalisation is the process of forming a noun from a verb or clause.

• Nominalisation of a clause

We need to keep the park so children have somewhere to play.
We need to keep the park *for children's recreation*.

- Nominalisation of a verb

> Because the President failed to remove the troops, many deaths occurred.
> The failure to remove the troops resulted in many deaths.

Nominalisations are a feature of particular types of writing, such as essays and technical writing that need to use abstract ideas and concepts. Arguments often use nominalisations as they can effectively remove agency and time from statements and therefore render the propositions more difficult to refute. Writing such as narratives, on the other hand, abstract language through the use of imagery (as discussed above) and generally make less use of nominalisations.

Nominalising clauses and verbs enable the removal of agency and time from processes, as in the President example above where the process of *failing* has become *failure*, a timeless, agentless phenomenon.

Nominalisations can be formed by simply using the present participle form of the verb, such as singing, running or killing, or by adding suffixes such as:

frustrate – frustration, nominalise – nominalisation	_ tion
argue – argument, govern – government	_ ment
refuse – refusal, propose – proposal	_ al

NOUNS

Nouns are words that name people, places, things and ideas. There are different types of nouns:

the vast majority are the names of classes of things and begin with a lower-case letter: *playground, park, tree, car*	Common nouns
name specific people, places and things and begin with a capital letter: *Sydney Harbour, Oliver Twist, Federal Government*	Proper nouns
name things that cannot be seen: *love, difference, idea*	Abstract nouns
name groups of things: *team, family, committee*	Collective nouns
name things that you cannot count: *gold, milk, sunshine, furniture*	Mass nouns

NOUN GROUP

A noun group is a group of words relating to, or adding information to, a noun. Noun groups usually consist of an article or determiner, plus one or more adjectives or adverbs and are often used in descriptions. Pre-modification of noun groups usually consists of an article plus one or more adjectives or adverbs. Adjectives are words that describe, evaluate or define the meaning of a noun. Adverbs can be used in noun groups to modify the meaning of or add extra information to adjectives. For example,

The dry, windswept, desert region has an extremely low rainfall.

The definite article	dry, adjective	windswept, adjective	desert classifying	region noun	has verb	an indefinite article	extremely adverb	low adjective	rainfall. noun

Noun groups can also have adjectival phrases or adjectival clauses embedded in them:

The problem *of poisonous pollution* is becoming an increasingly vexed issue.	Noun group with adjectival phrase embedded
The children *who arrive early to school* need supervision.	Noun group with adjectival clause embedded

OBJECT

The object is a noun (or noun group) that follows the verb without a preposition. To identify whether the noun (or noun group) following the verb is the object, use the following test. If the noun becomes the subject when the sentence is changed into the passive voice, then it is the object. For example,

The hikers were carrying a first aid kit.	Active voice
A first aid kit was being carried by the hikers.	Passive voice

Another test, but only for sentences in the active voice, is to ask the question: 'What is being affected by the verb?'

The hikers were carrying a first aid kit.
What was being carried? – a first aid kit.

Sentences can have more than one object. For example,

The park ranger showed the hikers the best route.

In this case there are two objects: one is the element that is being affected by the verb and is called a direct object. Ask, 'What did the park ranger show?' Answer – 'the best route' (the object can be identified by applying either of the above tests). In the above example there is another object; that is, the noun group that follows the verb (the hikers). Because this object is not directly related to the verb it is called an indirect object. To identify the indirect object, rewrite the sentence and add the word 'to' to the appropriate noun group and that will be the indirect object. For example,

The park ranger showed the best route to the hikers.

Not all verbs need an object; for example, verbs that describe behaviours like sleeping, running, jumping, snoring and so on (such verbs are known as intransitive verbs). For example,

The girl	shot	a goal.
subject	transitive verb	object
The girl	was running.	
subject	intransitive verb	

PERSON

In written English the choice of address significantly affects style. Address can be personal or impersonal, direct or indirect. Address is conveyed through the choice of person. The concept of person distinguishes, for example, the person speaking (first person), the person listening (second person), and the person being spoken about (third person). If a piece of writing is in the first person it has the effect of engaging the reader closely in a personal event, and is often used in narrative texts. For example,

I felt she was hiding something from me.

Use of second person is common to procedural texts. For example,

You should turn off the tap.

Third person removes the personal and puts a distance between the writer and the text, often giving the text a more formal style and objective tone. For example,

It is inappropriate for the government not to provide adequate funding.

The choice of person affects the type of pronouns that can be used.

I (me, my, mine) we (us, our, ours)	First person
you (your, yours)	Second person
he (him, his) she (her, hers) it (its) they (them, their, theirs)	Third person

PHRASE

A phrase (also known as a group) is a meaningful group of words that forms part of a sentence or clause. There are five types of phrase or group:

the difficult problem of supervision	Noun phrase
must not be seen	Verb phrase
seriously unmotivated	Adjectival phrase
quite happily	Adverbial phrase
before the event	Prepositional phrase

PREDICATE

This is a term in traditional grammar to identify the elements of a clause that complement the subject to form a statement.

PREPOSITIONS

Prepositions locate nouns, pronouns and noun groups in time, space or circumstance. For example,

In the morning *before* the bell rings, children like to play outside.

Some common prepositions are:

at	on	before	in	from
since	for	during	to	until
after	soon	by	into	onto
off	out	above	over	under
below	across	after	around	beside
between	down	past	near	through
without				

PRONOUNS

A pronoun stands in place of a noun, noun group or name. Pronouns refer to something that has been named (or is about to be named) and has already been written about. For example,

The park is a popular place. *It* is mostly used by children.

Pronouns provide a text with cohesion. Pronouns only work if they are not ambiguous (that is, there is a clear line of reference) and not used too repetitively. There are different types of pronouns:

she, he, you, etc.	Personal
mine, hers, yours, etc.	Possessive
himself, yourself, etc.	Reflexive
this, that, these, those	Demonstrative
each, any, some, all	Indefinite
who, which, what, whose, whom	Interrogative
who, which, that	Relative

QUESTION MARKS

Question marks are used to indicate that a sentence should be read as a direct question – *What time will you be returning?* Question marks are optional for indirect questions, requests, invitations or instructions – *Could I borrow your car. Won't you let me have it. Would you leave the keys in it.*

QUOTATION MARKS

Quotation marks, or inverted commas, identify words that are direct speech or spoken or written words belonging to people other than the writer. Quotation marks should not be used for indirect speech such as: *He said that I could use the car.* There is an increasing trend for single quotation marks ('...') to be used in place of double marks ("..."), although this is a matter of style. Double quotation marks are used for material quoted within single marks and vice versa if the material is quoted within double marks.

REFERENCE

Reference refers to the way in which information is introduced, maintained and expanded in a text. The use of pronouns (pronominal reference) is the most common way of maintaining reference without the clumsiness of continual naming. Pronouns are not used indefinitely, even if there is a clear line of reference to the noun as endless strings of pronouns make flat and uninteresting writing. Beginning a paragraph with a pronoun often makes it difficult for readers to determine the noun or name to which it is referring.

In this example there are two reference chains; one refers back to walruses (in bold), and the other refers back to hair (in italics).

When **walruses** are babies **they** have a lot of *hair* but when **they** grow up *it* falls out and **they** only have a little *bit* around the upper lip.

Reference chains:

When **walruses** are babies	walruses
they have a lot	they
of hair	hair
but when they grow up	they
it falls out	it
and they only have	they
a little bit around the upper lip	bit

Pronominal reference may be used, as in the above example, to refer to something that has already been established in the text, but it can also be used to refer to something that is to follow in the text.

The main thing being proposed here is *this*. That there is far too much time, money and effort being wasted in the production of unnecessary packaging.

SEMICOLONS

Semicolons are used within sentences to separate different though related pieces of information (main or contrasting clauses) – *Road traffic is a problem; it is particularly so near schools.* Many books and magazines now use dashes for this function. Semicolons are also used to separate complex items in a list.

SENTENCE

A sentence is a group of words that makes complete sense. It is marked in writing by beginning with a capital letter and ending with a full stop. There are four functions of sentences:

- making statements or declaratives

The girl	shot	a goal.
subject	verb	object

- asking questions or interrogatives

Did	the girl	shoot	a goal?
finite	subject	verb	object

- uttering commands or imperatives (generally the subject is ellipted)

Shoot	the goal
verb	object

- voicing exclamations or exclamatives

What a good goal	she	shot!
phrase	subject	verb

There are three types of sentences:

SIMPLE SENTENCES

A simple sentence has only one clause that makes complete sense. A simple sentence may include an embedded clause or one or more phrases.

The council should keep the local park.	Single main clause
The council should keep the local park *near the shopping centre.*	Main clause + adverbial phrase
The council *who are our representatives* should keep the park.	Main clause + embedded clause

An embedded clause (normally an adjectival or relative clause) provides extra information about the subject or object of a clause. For example,

| The council *who are our representatives* should keep the park. | Modifying the subject |
| The council should keep the park, *which is a great community asset.* | Modifying the object |

This feature of embedded clauses is that the clause is part of the structure of another clause and therefore does not have a coordinating or subordinating relationship with the main clause.

COMPOUND SENTENCES

In compound sentences there are two or more clauses that are coordinated or linked in such a way as to give each equal status as a statement. Compound sentences often share the same subject. For example,

The council reconsidered its decision and *kept the local park.*

The clauses in a compound sentence can be linked by the use of conjunctions or punctuation.

The council debated the issue *and* made a decision.
They debated enthusiastically; they made a decision.

Note how the conjunction 'and' is stated in the first example and ellipted in the second. Because compound sentences coordinate main or independent clauses equally, they most commonly use the additive conjunctions 'and' and 'or', or the contrastive conjunction, 'but'. The following are examples of other additive conjunctions that are sometimes used:

also	moreover
in addition	as well as
besides	furthermore

COMPLEX SENTENCES

A complex sentence consists of one main clause and one or more subordinate clauses. A subordinate clause refers to a clause that is providing a separate piece of information to the main clause but is dependent on the main clause to make sense. For example,

Pollution is a problem *because of its effect on the environment*. *If something isn't done soon*, the effects of pollution will be irreversible.

LEVELS OF COMPLEXITY

There can be levels of complexity within complex sentences. Within a dependent clause, for instance, there can be another dependent clause. For example, in the following complex sentence there is a main clause (**in bold**), a dependent clause in an adverbial relationship with the main clause (*in italics*), and a dependent clause (*<u>underlined italics</u>*) in an adverbial relationship with the first dependent clause.

If you want to survive the elements <u>when you go hiking</u>, **you should remember to bring along a drink, pocket knife, whistle, map, torch, compass, blanket and food.**

We could represent this complex structure with the diagram below:

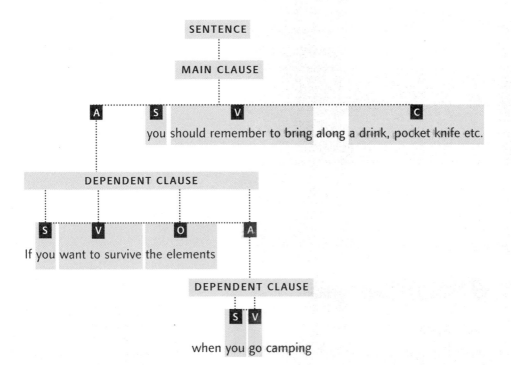

SUBJECT

The subject is the person or thing in a sentence or clause that 'operates' the verb. The easiest way to identify the subject is first to identify the verb and then ask the question, 'Who or what operates the verb?' For example, in the sentence '*Because of the complaints from children and their parents, the Council has decided to keep the park*', ask the question 'Who decided?' (the Council).

SUBJECT–VERB–OBJECT PATTERN

The order of elements in a sentence is relatively fixed in English in a subject–verb–object order (although there can be variations for stylistic purposes). The subject and the verb are obligatory and must be in concord (see Agreement). Even the simplest sentences have a subject and a verb, although in sentences like commands the subject is understood and, therefore, does not appear. The object can be optional as some verbs do not need an object (intransitive verbs) or the verb can be followed by an adverb, adverbial phrase or a complement which can be a noun or an adjective.

On most afternoons adverbial phrase	children subject	use verb	the park. object
During the meeting adverbial phrase	a lot of people subject	complained. intransitive verb	
They subject	complained verb	for the duration of the meeting. adverbial phrase	

SYNTAX

Syntax describes the grammatical relations between words as they are put together in phrases, clauses and sentences (syntactic structures). In the approach to grammar followed in this book the syntactic level considers the appropriate arrangement of words within the possibilities of English syntax.

TENSE

Tense refers to the capacity of verbs to express time. In English there are two ways of changing the forms of verbs to express different tenses:

- participles are additions made to verbs

verb + **ing**	playing, shopping	Continuous present
verb + **ed** or **en**	shopped, proven	Past

- auxiliaries are verbs like be, have and do that help the verb express time

I jump, I do jump, I am jumping*	Present
I jumped, I did jump, I was jumping*	Past
I shall/will jump, I shall/will be jumping*	Future
I have jumped, I have been jumping*	Present perfect
I had jumped, I had been jumping*	Past perfect
I shall/will have jumped, I shall/will have been jumping*	Future perfect

*The -ing form of each tense is called the continuous.

THEME/RHEME

Theme is a functional term that helps us to understand how information is communicated in sentences. When new information is introduced, it has to relate to what is already known by the reader. This normally means that the given or established information comes first, followed by the new or unknown information. Theme is therefore the grammatical name given to the first part of a sentence that establishes the known information shared between writer and readers. Although the theme is in the most prominent position in a sentence (it comes first), it is not necessarily the focus of the sentence. The focus is the new information being introduced, which is called the rheme. For example, note in the following how the emphasis of each sentence is the new information or rheme provided about the themes (ants).

An ant has three body parts.
Some ants have wings.
The queen ant lays the eggs.
Ants live in colonies.

Grammatically, theme is a useful category for helping students to organise information at a sentence level so that it is thematically linked to the overall message of the text (metatheme).

VERB

Verbs are the dynamic element in sentences and clauses. They provide the movement or action, or a sense of what is happening. A complete sentence (unless it is a minor utterance such as Yes. or Good morning.) will have a finite verb; that is, a word that changes its form to mark tense and agreement of person and number. Verbs are always attached to nouns or pronouns. Different types of verbs are used, depending on the purpose of the text. The writing could feature action verbs (the traditional 'doing words'), mental verbs (words that express feeling or thinking), or relational verbs (which set up relationships between one thing and another thing or state or attribute). In other words, they provide the sense of movement in time and space in the relationship between one thing and another, or one thing and its circumstance or attributes. Verbs do not exist in language on their own; they must always be attached to a noun.

From a formal perspective, there are two types of verbs: full verbs and auxiliary verbs. Full verbs are divided into regular verbs and irregular verbs. Regular verbs share the same form when dealing with tense in a verb group.

- The base form, talk, used for the first and second person present tense.
- The -s form, talks, used in the third person present tense.
- The -ing form, talking, used for the present continuous participle.
- The -ed form, talked, used for the past tense and past participle.

Irregular verbs have -s forms and -ing forms that are regular but have varying forms for the past tense and past participle. For example,

Write, writing, wrote
Give, giving, gave
Become, becoming, became

VERB GROUPS

Verbs on their own tell us what is 'going on', but they often need other elements to locate the 'goings on' in either time, probability or manner, or combinations of these. These elements of a verb group can be identified as verb, auxiliaries and adverbs, as in:

Lara	has	magnificently	driven	the ball over the bowler's head.
	auxiliary	adverb	verb + past participle	

In this case, has magnificently driven is a verb group that locates the act of driving in time (has) and manner (magnificently).

Similarly, a verb group can locate an action in probability, time, and manner as in:

The batsman	might	have	slightly	edged	the ball past the keeper.
	probability	time	adverb	verb + past participle	

In this case *might have slightly edged* is a verb group that expresses some probability about whether the batsman touched the ball with his bat.

PARTICIPLES

Participles are additions made to verbs to help locate them in time:

verb + ing	Continuous present; for example, playing, shopping
verb + en or ed	Past; for example, shopped, proven.

Adding participles to verbs enables them to be used as adjectives or nouns.

I was *shopping* for a present.	Participle
We went to the *shopping* centre.	Adjective
The *shopping* was a great success.	Noun

FINITE VERBS

A finite verb is one that expresses time and has a definite tense and mood (indicative or imperative).

The park *opens* from 9 a.m.	Present indicative
The park *opened* from 9 a.m.	Past indicative
Open the park at 9 a.m.	Present imperative

The first element of a verb group is the finite element:

The traffic *is* moving.
The traffic *has* moved.
The traffic *may* have moved.

Non-finite verbs have no time element; for example, *'to walk, walking'*.

The traffic was seen *speeding* past the school.
The traffic was observed *to speed* past the school.

AUXILIARY VERBS

Auxiliary verbs are helping verbs. They regularly help full verbs to specify and express time and probability/obligation. Auxiliary verbs are divided into primary auxiliaries (be, have, do) and modal auxiliaries (can, may, will, shall, must, ought to, need, dare). In verb groups that express probability and time, the modal auxiliary comes first.

The girl *has* been playing netball.	Time
The girl *must* have shot a goal.	Probability
The girl *must* shoot a goal.	Obligation

The 'operator' is the functional term given to the finite element of a verb group. Auxiliary verbs become the operator when they occur as the first verb in a finite verb group.

FUNCTIONAL ACCOUNTS OF VERBS

There are two ways of looking at the relationship between the syntactical elements in clauses and sentences. One way is to see the function of a verb as expressing a dynamic relationship between the subject and object or complement (either a thing or a circumstance). So, for instance, in a simple sentence like *Lara drove the ball*, the verb *drove* acts as a dynamic process between the subject doing the hitting (Lara) and the object of hitting (the ball). Clearly, the verb is expressing a dynamic action going on 'out there' and is functioning as an 'action verb'.

Lara	drove	the ball.
subject	action	object

In grammar, this account of the role of verbs in sentences is called transitivity. When verbs act in this way they are said to be transitive. In other words, they are representing the movement from the person doing the hitting or driving to the thing that is affected by the hitting or driving. Not all verbs, however, are transitive – they can represent something dynamic happening, but it happens without affecting anything or anyone. For example,

> Last night it rained.
> The children were running.

When verbs do not have an object they are said to be intransitive. Many verbs can be both transitive and intransitive. For example:

| The girls are playing. | Intransitive |
| The girls are playing netball. | Transitive |

FUNCTIONAL CATEGORIES OF VERBS

Apart from knowing the formal characteristics of verbs and verb groups, it is important to understand what verbs are 'doing' semantically. Not all verbs are 'doing words' or simply representing actions. In many types of writing, only a minority of verbs represent concrete actions. Different types of verbs are used, depending on what we are doing with the language. For example, if giving a series of instructions, action verbs would tend to dominate. When describing the appearance of something, relational verbs are used, but when describing behaviours, action verbs are used. For this reason we need a way of categorising verbs that can help students to identify the appropriate verbs for the purpose of their writing.

For the purposes of school writing, verbs can be categorised into three types: action, mental and relational. These categories are particularly useful when teaching students to apply the appropriate writing for the purpose and audience of texts. The traditional definition of verbs as 'doing words' is often less than adequate, particularly when students develop as writers where they make less use of action verbs and greater use of relational, mental and metaphoric action verbs.

ACTION VERBS

Action verbs refer to the traditional notion of verbs as 'doing words'; that is, verbs that refer to concrete actions and can be identified by the question, 'Can this verb be done?' Action verbs are common in spoken language and are therefore common in the writing of younger students, particularly in writing that refers to concrete events, people or things in their world.

Action verbs predominantly occur in texts where actions or behaviours are being described and/or recounted. For example,

> Snails *slide* when they move.
> The walrus *eats* shellfish, which they *remove* with their tusks.
> Before we *went* on a boat we *bought* oranges and my mother *brought* her jewels with her too.
> She *told* me that we *are going* to grandmother's house *to visit* her.

Action verbs often refer to abstract or metaphorical actions or processes. Metaphoric action verbs are useful for abstracting or adding more complex or descriptive layers of meaning to sentences. For example,

> The crowd *spilled* out into the street.

MENTAL VERBS

Mental verbs refer to things that happen to or are done by humans within themselves – things like thinking and feeling. In this sense they are 'doing words', but are not overt actions. They express feelings, attitudes, ideas and so on, and are subjective rather than objective.

Mental verbs are common in genres such as arguing and narrating, and are also used in personal descriptions, but are not a feature of technical descriptions. Science is generally concerned with objective descriptions of the world rather than with subjective attitudes.

Mental verbs are useful for qualifying facts and opinions; for example, *Many people think that*, is often more effective in an argument than *It is a fact that...* The latter, by being an absolute statement, forces the reader into either total agreement or disagreement, while the former allows room for argument.

> My big bear's name is Snowy. I like him so much.
> Many people feel that too much packaging is a waste of natural resources.
> It would appear that too much food has been wasted.

RELATIONAL VERBS

Relational verbs are used extensively in most types of writing. At a basic level they are fundamental to all types of description; they express meanings about what things 'are' and what they 'have'. The main way of doing this involves the verbs 'to be' and 'to have'. As a general rule, when using writing for the expression of knowledge, it is easier to deal with processes and concepts in their noun forms. Here relational verbs have a fundamental role in setting up relationships in sentences between one thing and another. For example,

> People today are making their packages environmentally friendly.
> The manufacture of packaging today is more environmentally friendly.

On the one hand, relational verbs are used to show the attributes of a thing or element, and on the other, they can be used to identify it. Each of these relational verbs can be categorised as intensive (x is y), circumstantial (x is at y) and possessive (x has y).

Identifying types are distinguishable from attributive types in that they are reversible. For example,

> Iman is the goal shooter.
> The goal shooter is Iman.

Attributive types are not reversible. For example,

> Iman is a good shot.

but not

> A good shot is Iman.

Possessive-type relational verbs can use the verb 'to have' or the verb 'to be'. For example,

> Iman has the ball.

or

> The ball is Iman's.

Both attributive and possessive types can use the verb 'to have'. For example,

Iman has a good shooting action.	Attributive
Iman has the ball in her hand.	Possessive

Relationships in sentences are not always represented by the verbs 'to be' and 'to have'. There are many other verbs that can be used to express relationships. For example,

produces	leads to	allows	shows
represents	exemplifies	creates	results in
brings about	initiates	culminates	gives rise to
reflects	manifests	discloses	expresses
shows	generates	contributes	reveals
means	symbolises	indicates	becomes

CHAPTER 3

PEDAGOGIC PRINCIPLES IN TEACHING AND ASSESSING WRITING

In this chapter we focus on the teaching and learning of genre and grammar. The approach used here considers the teaching/learning of genre and grammar across all student age levels and across all curriculum areas. It highlights a set of five pedagogic principles that should be considered in the teaching of four integrated elements: content/language, structure, grammar and assessment. This approach to teaching and learning language within the context of the knowledge of the learning areas allows teachers and students to share a common understanding about the role of language in learning, whereby the whole process becomes far more effective and efficient, resulting in significant improvement in student writing.

PAST APPROACHES

Approaches to the teaching of writing have changed markedly over the last 30 years. These changes relate not only to curriculum, or what is taught, but also to pedagogy, or how the curriculum is conceived and implemented in classrooms. While teaching practice at any particular time is never homogeneous, since teachers necessarily employ a range of strategies to best cater for the needs of their students, there has been a shift in emphasis away from more teacher-directed methodologies to student-centred and computer-assisted learning. In practice, this has resulted in a reduction in whole-class instruction and a greater focus on group-based learning strategies. These latter approaches are closely allied with progressivist educational ideals. Based on a critique and rejection of the perceived authoritarianism of traditional education, progressivism is essentially student-centred. Learning is conceived as a function of a child's experience, a process that should be fostered by teachers through encouragement and an enriched learning environment with teacher intervention discouraged. In fact, in its more extreme forms, progressivism actively discouraged any sense of teacher intervention and it was this ideological environment that helped enable the movements of 'whole language' and 'process writing'.

This perspective on education proved highly influential during the 1970s and 1980s, and to some extent still frames the dominant discourses around pedagogic practice today. Progressivism meshed well with the approach to language that was favoured at this time. Drawing heavily on psycholinguistic theory, language was conceived as a natural and largely individual phenomenon and so rather than approaching the teaching of English on a corporate basis through whole-class instruction, group-based learning became a dominant methodology. This does not simply mean the move to students sitting in groups, as opposed to rows of desks, but learning based around group activities. Group-based learning was considered to have an additional benefit in that it allowed greater collaboration and therefore talk among students. It was felt that through talk students would naturally acquire competence in all language modes. Progressivist literacy pedagogies made little distinction between speech and writing, as exemplified in the 1974 New South Wales Language Syllabus, which declared that 'Language learning occurs as a series of related experiences in which one use of language leads naturally to others' (New South Wales, Department of Education 1974, p. 4). This perspective on language learning was replicated in other states of Australia and reflected a general trend in the teaching of English in other Western countries. As a result of this there

seemed no real need to teach grammar and the variabilities of textual form as appropriate usage would result from verbal interaction
in the classroom leading onto a seamless engagement in the writing
process. There were many influential voices at this time stressing this
point, most notably Krashen (1981, 1984) who argued that it was
useless, if not dangerous, to explicitly teach writing and grammar.

These changes in pedagogic practice had a major impact on the
role of the teacher with emphasis placed more on the facilitation of
learning rather than classroom instruction. This perspective on language leaning came under the scrutiny of a range of linguistic and
educational researchers in the latter part of the 1980s; in particular,
by those advocating a genre-based approach to teaching writing
(Reid 1987; Richardson 1991; Cope, Kalantzis, Kress, Martin and
Murphy 1993). These critics, ourselves included (Knapp 1989;
Watkins 1990), not only called for a new curriculum focus on
grammar and the genres of school writing, but for a more explicit
pedagogy to support its implementation. In 1988 a three-stage
model, or curriculum cycle, was developed by the New South Wales
Metropolitan East Disadvantaged School Program as a result of
research by Martin (1987) and Rothery (1986). This model involved
modelling the context and text under examination, additional activities in preparation for the joint construction of this text, and then
finally a stage of independent construction of the text by students,
as shown below in figure 3.1(Callaghan and Rothery 1988).

Apart from Martin and Rothery's classroom research this model
drew extensively on the work of theorists of language learning such
as Vygotsky, Halliday and Painter, and gave emphasis to the need for
greater teacher direction in learning to write. Vygotsky, the notable
Soviet social psychologist, stated that 'Instruction is one of the prin-
cipal sources of the schoolchild's concepts and is also a powerful
force in directing their evolution; it determines the fate of {their}
total mental development' (Vygotsky 1996, p. 157). Vygotsky made
this claim on the basis of his work in child psychology that critiqued
Piaget's rigid developmental model. He developed what he termed
the Zone of Proximal Development or ZPD, describing the gap
between a child's actual development determined by independent
problem-solving and his or her potential development achieved
when assisted (Vygotsky 1996, p. 187). The form of assistance
Vygotsky intended was not simply that provided by peers, but by
teachers explicitly directing a child's learning. Vygotsky was highly

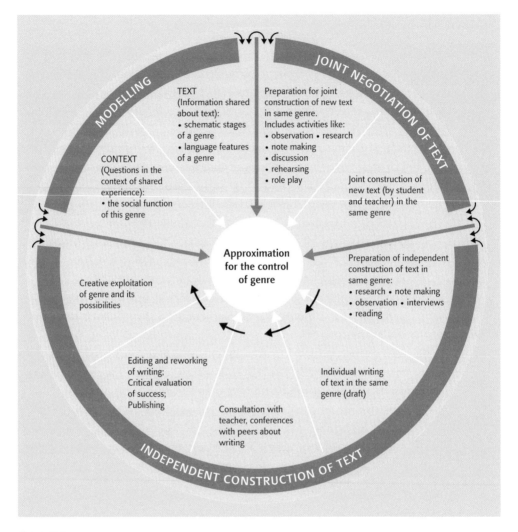

FIGURE 3.1
The curriculum cycle (Callaghan and Rothery 1988, p.39)

critical of the progressivist education movement that was influential in the Soviet Union during the 1920s (van der Veer and Valsiner 1991, p. 53). This focus on 'directed' learning is also evident in studies of child language development. The research of Halliday (1975) and Painter (1991) demonstrated the ways in which parents and caregivers actively support young children in their construction of spoken texts scaffolding their language use. In utilising aspects of these different theorists' work, together with a more explicit focus on text and grammar, it was intended that the curriculum cycle of modelling, joint construction and independent construction would provide a more effective approach to teaching students to write.

In many respects this was the case and the curriculum cycle and its distinctive stages have proved extremely influential. References to 'modelling' and 'joint construction' in the teaching of writing can be found in syllabuses across Australia and elsewhere. Yet despite its wide acceptance, there are some concerns about how the approach has fared in practice and its overall effectiveness in improving students' writing (Callaghan, Knapp and Noble, 1993; Luke, 1994; Freedman, 1994). One disturbing trend, foreseen by Kress (1993), is the tendency for this approach to teaching text to simply result in students reproducing a set of textual types. Through the process of modelling, joint construction and then independently constructing a text there is little possibility for creative manipulation or examination of the variability of textual form. In the original version of the curriculum cycle, shown above, the final stage of independent construction encouraged 'the creative exploitation of the genre and its possibilities' (Callaghan and Rothery 1988, p. 39). In practice, however, this rarely, if ever, was undertaken, and in syllabus documents and curriculum support material, both departmental and commercially produced, the focus is clearly on replicating a set of mandated textual types. Even if consideration is given to the point made in the original version of the curriculum cycle, the potential for experimenting with text within this model is quite limited. This is not simply a function of its stages of curriculum implementation, but also the theory of genre on which it is based (Martin 1992).

With genre understood as a text type or product, the pedagogy underpinning the model is largely geared towards reproduction. This process of simply replicating dominant forms is not only criticised here due to the limitations it places on students' understanding of text, but also because it often leads to many students producing very poor attempts at writing these textual types. This is largely a result of the emphasis a product notion of genre gives to structure over grammar. Many teachers simply focus on the schematic stages of each text that are generally displayed in classrooms as a set of textual formulas and give little, if any, attention to the grammar generic to each text. While there are exceptions to this, with some teachers effectively modelling the grammar of each text type, many simply have their students identify grammatical features, reminiscent of traditional strategies of parsing and analysis, or conduct editing activities with a simplistic syntactic or rule-based orientation. While there is value in this approach to grammar, its focus is not about how to write different types of texts. The grammatical foundations of the generic stages of texts seem to be either overlooked or given insufficient treatment. Different textual forms are generally only discussed in terms of their structural features. As Williams (1993, p. 217) remarks, however, 'To use only description at the level of discourse structure, such as the schematic structure of genre, is to run the risk of cutting genre description adrift from their anchorage in the grammatical patterning of language and therefore to have them floating about in educational contexts unrelated to their purposes and in the living of life'. It is at the level of grammar that much generic variation occurs. Teachers need to address this, not only if they intend to have their students play with generic form, but even if they simply expect their students to faithfully reproduce a textual type.

Another way in which grammar is seemingly addressed is through the process of jointly constructing a text. This strategy of demonstrating correct grammar through teachers transcribing students' responses on the board, with modification where necessary, simplifies the complex movement from speech to writing. While perhaps a useful first step, the actual grammatical manipulation involved in the teacher's reworking of their students' verbal responses needs to be made more explicit with students examining these processes in their own writing to effectively reproduce a particular type of text. In some respects the minimal emphasis placed on teaching grammar is a function of its erasure from the curriculum over an extended period of years, resulting in many teachers simply not possessing the requisite grammatical understanding to teach it to their students. While this is of course a factor, it is primarily the product orientation of the approach itself that allows for minimal treatment of the grammar generic to each of the text types it privileges.

Ironically, what has also proved problematic with the implementation of the text-type approach to genre theory is the degree of teacher direction it requires. As already discussed, the theory underpinning the curriculum cycle promotes a pedagogic stance of greater teacher intervention and scaffolded learning (Hammond 2001). While these are pedagogic ideals to which we also adhere, this model was simply superimposed over a progressivist paradigm of teaching and learning that tended to neutralise these aspects of the approach. Group-based and independent learning strategies, and the perspective that the role of the teacher is more to facilitate than to instruct, have become so firmly entrenched in contemporary classrooms that the degree of teacher input and guidance actually required for effective implementation has been minimised. The curriculum cycle is often reduced to a pedagogy of simply show, tell and do (Watkins 1997, 1999). Once a teacher has shown students a particular text type, told them about its generic stages and conducted a joint trial construction, students are then expected to produce the text. Often this is the full extent of the guidance in writing the various text types itemised in syllabus documents. The assumption is made that students have then amassed the necessary expertise to apply different content knowledge to replicating other versions of the same text.

What is missing here is any focus on what could be termed the 'bodily' aspects of learning; namely, that writing is a practice requiring iterative performance to achieve competence. Models such as the curriculum cycle seem to mask the incremental steps implicit in each of their macro stages: steps that should be characterised by considerable teacher–student interaction; that is, the inter-subjective engagement in the process of learning provided on a whole-class, group and individual basis. In more concrete terms this involves detailed teacher explanation and the guiding of students through the completion of tasks targeting smaller facets of what contributes to the production of textual form – the ability to manipulate the intricate patterning of the grammatical resources of language. The process of learning to write does not simply require cognition of a text's generic structure, it involves the embodiment of a complex set of knowledge and skills that then allows for a student to give more mindful consideration to the production of text. To quote Bourdieu (2000, p. 141), 'We learn bodily'. The bodily dimension of writing, that is sitting and labouring to construct a text, what is habituated technique in proficient writers, is generally taken for granted within contemporary literacy pedagogy. Being able to write and write well, however, requires students' bodies to be attuned to the dynamics of writing. Teachers, therefore, need to devote considerable time to developing students' grammatical understanding through integrated units of work that examine aspects of grammar and text in sustained, repeated yet varied ways.

This is not only undertaken in terms of whole-class instruction and then individual application with teacher support – although these are necessary aspects of what we consider to be effective pedagogic practice. Group work also has an important role to play. This, however, is not so much in terms of its progressivist rationale of encouraging talk and student-centred learning. Effectively, organised group work is probably best used at different stages of a unit of work to allow students to consolidate knowledge and skills, rather than as a methodology with which to teach foundational aspects of learning to write. In the initial stages of learning about a new concept, students require time for sustained and concentrated engagement. Writing is itself a relatively disciplined activity and while discussion and working with peers is important, so is the time to individually reflect on work and independently complete a task. Through this process, particularly with the emphasis shifted from genre as product to genre as process, students develop skills that not only allow them to replicate a singularly generic textual type more effectively, but to construct multi-generic texts and to play with the technologies of genre, text and grammar in a creative fashion.

GENRE TEXT AND GRAMMAR APPROACH

In the approach used here for teaching and learning genre, text and grammar we have avoided using either a curriculum cycle or model of sequential steps. While we have done this in the past, we now feel that approaching pedagogy in this way has a tendency to be reductionist in practice (Knapp 1992; Knapp and Watkins 1994). What we feel is important, and is a more appropriate guide for teachers, is to outline the integrated elements required for teaching and learning genre and grammar, and to frame these with a set of principles for effective pedagogic practice. In our discussion of each of these elements, certain strategies are referred to but these do not constitute a pedagogy in themselves. 'Pedagogy' is quite a difficult term to define. In a recent New South Wales Department of Education and Training document drawing on a range of research, pedagogy is considered to be 'the art and science of teaching' (New South Wales Department of Education and Training 2003, p. 4). It is a term that 'recognises that how one teaches is inseparable from what one teaches, from what and how one assesses and from how one learns' (2003 p. 4). While we would agree with these comments, pedagogy also involves far more than this, something that is often left unsaid, but which implicitly underpins all teaching practice; that is, a pedagogy is always grounded by a particular philosophy which frames a teacher's conceptions of his or her role in the classroom and perspective on the ways in which the students learn. It is for this reason that pedagogies can be termed traditional or progressive. These terms relate to particular educational philosophies that influence the different facets that constitute a pedagogy. While progressivism still appears the dominant paradigm of teaching and learning, alternate perspectives have emerged to not only challenge progressivism, but also critique the binary of traditional and progressive philosophies in education. It is in fact our intention to move beyond progressivism to what could be termed a *post-progressivist* philosophy of teaching and learning – a pedagogy quite distinct from either traditionalism or progressivism. The key principles of this pedagogy are outlined below. (See Figure 3.2 pp. 88).

PEDAGOGIC PRINCIPLES: TEACHING AND LEARNING OF GENRE AND GRAMMAR

THE MOVEMENT FROM CONCRETE TO ABSTRACT KNOWLEDGE

As much as possible, it is important to commence the treatment of new knowledge within a unit of work with what is familiar, concrete and observable before moving students to more abstract understandings. In many respects this is a key pedagogic tenet, but one that is often neglected in practice. Examples of how this may be undertaken are briefly outlined in the following typical units of work:

- Minibeasts: students could first observe and describe the appearance and behaviour of ants and other insects, and assign common-sense names to what they look like and what they do, before considering technical terms and the use of more sophisticated language.
- Fairytales: students could read and be read fairy tales from different cultures to provide a context for examining traditional narrative structure.

- Discovering the past: students could conduct their own archae-
  ological dig in a sand box and explain what they did before
  thinking about layers of civilisation in an actual site.
- Technology – papermaking: students could make their own
  paper before writing a set of instructions, or possibly an explanation, on how to make paper and then compare this process with
  commercial papermaking.

The possibilities are endless but important to consider. This movement from concrete to abstract does not only relate to conceptual
understanding, but also to the language used to process these
understandings. The notion of concrete also applies to the use of
commonsense terminology and spoken language that should be
used as a resource for moving students towards the abstract world
of technical terminology and written language. Also, some genres
are more useful when dealing with concrete representations and are
therefore fundamental in building understanding through language.
In units of work it is important therefore to start with genres that
concretely represent what students have experienced or observed;
for example, genres that define and describe their world such as
describing and explaining.

ITERATIVE PRACTICE

Students learn by doing, but not simply through one-off activities.
They require considerable yet varied practice to develop an
understanding of all aspects of writing, not only grammatical and
structural knowledge of text, which is our focus here, but also
spelling, punctuation and syntax, which are vital to writing effectively. Through iterative practice students come to habituate the
skills that then give them the 'cognitive space' to reflect upon the
writing process. In doing so they gain greater competency and can
begin to creatively manipulate text. This notion of making certain
skills and knowledge automatic seems to be well understood in
learning to read where it is taken as given that if students can
process text rapidly they have a greater capacity for comprehension and reflection – a necessary factor in developing critical
understanding. This same principle can be applied to writing. If
students acquire automaticity in lower order skills they can then
improve their creative and critical capacities in the production of
text.

CONCENTRATED TREATMENT OF KNOWLEDGE AND SKILLS

Students do not only learn through iterative practice they learn through sustained application to set tasks. To be able to do this, teachers need to give concentrated treatment to knowledge and skills in their teaching of units of work, devoting time and attention to content knowledge and language. This not only has implications for programming, in that units of work cannot be rushed, it also impacts upon the particular pedagogic modes that teachers utilise in classrooms. Ample time needs to be given to allow students to work individually and apply the concepts examined in class in their own writing. The balance of whole-class instruction, group work and independent work needs to be carefully considered, particularly given that many students do not have the opportunity or inclination to work on their own in their home environment. The ability to work and write independently should not be taken for granted, it is a skill that needs to be learned and appropriately modelled within a classroom context.

EXPLICIT AND SYSTEMATIC INSTRUCTION

Prior to students applying knowledge, either on a group or individual basis, they need to have a good grasp of what they are required to do. This is achieved through explicit and systematic instruction. These terms are used more and more often within current educational discourse and seem to be acquiring a certain legitimacy with regard to presenting an alternative to the minimal interventionist stance of progressivism. By 'explicit' we mean that teachers need to be quite specific about what they are teaching. The notion of 'explicitness' is especially important in teaching writing as there are many different facets to the writing process and they can be overlooked. Each needs to be singled out for examination with a class and then applied within the context of the unit of work that students are studying. For example, it is not enough to ask students to write in a more descriptive way within a unit of work focusing on narrative. Depending on a child's particular stage of learning, teachers need to unpack the grammatical resources required to write more descriptively. This could involve examining different descriptive devices such as adjectives, adverbs, building more complex noun groups, using simile and metaphor, alliteration and metaphoric verbs. This could be undertaken through separate activities and by then applying them to students' own writing. The term 'systematic' requires that the treatment of each of these aspects of genre and grammar is staged appropriately. The examination of one particular concept needs to relate to and build upon another, resulting in an accumulation of knowledge and skills that enables more effective application.

These two terms are suggestive of a particular philosophy of teaching and learning which puts emphasis on teachers directing and scaffolding their students' learning. It views the teacher as not only a facilitator of learning, but as one whose instructional techniques are central to learning. This relates very much to Vygotsky's perspective that 'instruction usually precedes development' (Vygotsky 1996, p. 184). The notion of teacher directedness should not be conceived as indicative of a teacher-centred pedagogy. Perspectives of learning as being either 'teacher-centred' or 'student-centred' tend to bifurcate the learning process, which is dependent upon a dynamic of teaching and learning. The teaching/learning relationship, however, is not an equal one. This does not mean that the relationship is unidirectional with the teacher simply directing the child's learning, but it does acknowledge a power differential, which is not simply a function of the teacher's institutional position, but, rather, a result of their greater understanding. The teacher, therefore, through his or her own accumulated knowledge and skills, has a responsibility to guide and support a child's learning. The teacher may direct the students' learning, but, so too, the students' learning will, and should, direct the teacher's teaching. It is for this reason that teachers need a range of assessment strategies and instruments to assist in this diagnostic aspect of pedagogy.

DIAGNOSTIC ASSESSMENT

In the current context of outcomes-based assessment, teachers use a range of procedures to determine if students have achieved particular skills and knowledge. However, there are various perspectives on assessment, with many being misunderstood and poorly applied, especially in relation to the assessment of writing for diagnostic purposes.

Formative assessment covers a range of everyday teaching practices such as observation and questioning. Other techniques, such as photocopied worksheets with exercises and activities, enable teachers to gather valuable formative assessment data. Successful diagnostic assessment practices require teachers to systematically analyse the type of formative assessment information they are gathering. Using worksheets that target particular skills and knowledge relevant to the instructional content of the unit of work enables teachers to assess the effectiveness of their teaching and make accurate judgements on whether revision is required or students are ready to move on to the next stage of the unit.

Diagnostic assessment is also important when conducting summative assessments. In particular, when setting a summative assessment like a writing task it is important that the criteria used for assessing the writing adequately cover the range of generic, structural and grammatical features that formed the instructional content of the unit of work. At the end of this chapter we will outline a basic framework for assessing student writing intended to provide teachers with a range of diagnostic information on student writing performance.

These five pedagogic principles – the movement from concrete to abstract knowledge, iterative practice, concentrated treatment of knowledge and skills, explicit and systematic instruction, and diagnostic assessment – need to be considered in relation to the four integrated elements of teaching and learning genre and grammar: content/language, structure, grammar and assessment. Although it seems unavoidable, there is no real intention in the diagram below to represent these elements as a sequence of steps. Despite the use of two-sided arrows, there appears to be inadvertent staging of these four elements. While it is generally the case that a unit of work will commence with some treatment of disciplinary content we want to stress that this should not be simply at an initial stage followed by an examination of structure and grammar and then concluding with an assessment task. Treatment of content should occur throughout a unit of work and be interspersed with an examination of the structure and grammar of the genre(s) under focus. Together with this, assessment needs to be diagnostic, whether it is formative and occurring throughout the teaching of a unit of work, or summative, to make comparative judgements on student performance.

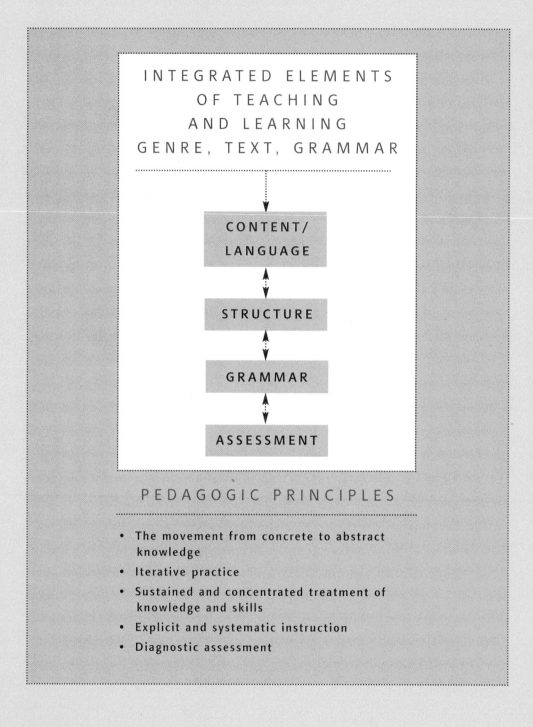

FIGURE 3.2

Integrated elements of teaching and
learning genre and grammar

CONTENT/LANGUAGE

DESIGNING UNITS OF WORK

Language is often seen as one thing and knowledge as another, with the relationship at best seen as a transparent one. What we often see in textbooks and other curriculum materials, for instance, is that language is treated as an almost transparent medium in the overall learning process, and consequently there is a careless use of genres and grammar. For example, science books that shift from explanation to narrative to instruction, with the grammar moving backwards and forwards between personal and impersonal voice, make heavy language demands on the reader. This can be the same case in units of work if careful attention is not given to making close connections between content knowledge and the language used to process it. Theme-based units often comprise an eclectic mix of activities that relate to similar content, but which give little attention to language. In completing these activities, students shift between describing, narrating, instructing, for example, with no time devoted to developing competency in a particular generic process. In designing units of work it is important to try and 'match' content with the particular genre(s) under examination. For example, a unit of work on the environment lends itself to a focus on arguing, a unit of work on space could focus on either describing or explaining or both, depending on the stage of learning of a class and their familiarity with each genre. Units of work on rules and diet might begin with some describing and explaining in dealing with aspects of content, but could give then give emphasis to instructing as a focus genre. In order to deal comprehensively with the relationship between knowledge and language, the treatment of content should not be rushed. When planning teaching/learning activities, teachers should think about the language activities that will reinforce the learning processes, giving attention to the pedagogic principles outlined above, in particular the movement from concrete to abstract knowledge. After initially dealing with knowledge in this way teachers can then conduct activities that move students towards more abstract understanding of a topic. These activities often involve reading and research, and it is important to consider the following when doing so.

READING MODELS

Once students have developed independent reading skills, the following strategies are designed to make explicit connections between the processes of reading and writing; in particular, they aim to promote the practices that will produce critical readers.

- Choose texts that are generically 'simple'. Texts that are not clear in their purpose or which shift almost aimlessly between genres can provide poor models for student writing.
- Use the text as an object to be pulled apart and examined. Question the untouchability of the printed word. Show students that reading is an active process of unpacking all elements of a text.
- Do several readings, each time examining different aspects, such as:

purpose　Why is the text written like this?
　　　　　Who is the audience?
　　　　　Who was it written by?

message　What is the text about?
　　　　　What are its main themes?

structure　Are different parts of the text doing different jobs?
　　　　　Is language used differently in each stage?

grammar　What type of language is being used to do each job?
　　　　　For example, what words are used to describe here?
　　　　　What are they describing?
　　　　　What type of words are they?

RESEARCH/NOTE-TAKING

- Collaborate with the school or local librarian in conducting a research lesson in the library.
- Assist students by providing research sheets scaffolded to accommodate the generic structure of the text they will later produce.
- Show how to collect relevant information in point form. The format of the research sheets will assist in this task.

STRUCTURE

This element looks at the way texts are structured in distinctive steps or stages to achieve their purposes. Students need to be provided with an explicit framework or scaffold for their writing, with the aim of having them achieve an appreciable degree of success with their written texts. By focusing on the generic structure, students can concentrate on organising the content knowledge into a functional framework or structure. Remember that the aim here is to build students' confidence in producing functionally coherent texts. This should not be undertaken as a one-off activity, but over a number of lessons throughout a unit so students can develop the complexity of their texts by integrating aspects of the grammar that they have also considered. Once students are confident at writing in a particular genre, then introduce other structural elements such as text organisation.

MODELLING GENERIC STRUCTURE

Show how each stage of a genre has an important function in the text's overall purpose. For example, show how in the genre of arguing, an exposition moves through the following stages:

Thesis	1	Statement of thesis
	2	Preview
Arguments	3	Point for
	4	Elaboration
	5	Point
	6	Elaboration
	7	Counterpoint
	8	Elaboration
Conclusion	9	Summary
	10	Reiteration of thesis

Point out how some stages are obligatory and others are optional; for example, the repetition of the arguments stage in an exposition. Analyse each stage of model texts in terms of how each achieves its generic purpose.

MODELLING TEXT ORGANISATION

- Show how features of text organisation or grammar such as titles, headings and paragraphs are a part of the generic structure of a text.
- Look at the role of a topic sentence in a paragraph.
- Show how paragraphs are identified by an indent or space.
- Model ways of opening an introductory paragraph.

- Model ways of:
  - introducing other viewpoints
  - summing up
  - introducing recommendations
  - writing about cause and effect
  - writing about the significance of something
  - expressing judgements in writing
  - writing about the significance of a situation or event.

SCAFFOLDING STUDENT TEXTS

Depending on the language development of the students, be prepared to be very explicit the first time students attempt this task.

- Write up the generic structure on a board or overhead transparency.
- In point form, have students contribute to each generic stage, using the content knowledge/language already developed.
- Incorporate features of text organisation appropriate for the genre.
- Provide handouts with the generic structure framework for students to fill out.
- Ask students to write their texts based on the generic structure/ content framework.
- Cut up texts, placing topic sentences in one pile and paragraphs in another. Ask students to match each.

GRAMMAR

While it is recognised that students have competence in many spoken genres, which is a fundamental step in learning to write, this does not mean that moving from speech to writing is simply a matter of transcribing speech. Students learn to write through the medium of writing. They learn the grammar of writing through understanding the way that their own writing works. As with structure, the treatment of grammar needs to be interspersed within a unit of work to slowly develop students' competency in utilising different grammatical resources in their own writing.

- Have students write simple, short, well-defined writing tasks; for example, ask students to describe what they can see.
- Compare and contrast the different approaches to this task.
- Give students the grammatical names and functions of the

language they have used for this task; for example, verbs, nouns and adjectives.

- Have students use these techniques in another description or to enhance a narrative.

WRITING/EDITING

At first have students write their texts stage by stage; for example, if writing a description, first write a topic classification.

- Compare and contrast the different approaches to this task.
- Build on the grammatical names and functions of the language they have used for the task; for example, classifications always use relational verbs.
- Have students (individually, in pairs, or in groups) use their knowledge of genre and grammar to rebuild or edit what they have written.
- Gradually apply these processes to whole texts.

ASSESSMENT

The 'genre and grammar' approach proposed here offers an objective approach to assessment based on the particular generic, structural and grammatical features of genres. For example, the features of writing using the genre of describing will be significantly different to those of arguing or narrating. In the following chapters we will identify the salient features of each of the genres and apply these to a systematic methodology to assessing student writing in each of the genres.

The assessment methodology uses the following groups of categories for all of the genres, but identifies relevant criteria within each group to objectively identify levels of achievement or non-achievement.

GENERIC FEATURES

- Genre Criteria in this group consider whether the writing successfully uses the appropriate genre for the task. For example, if the task requires an argument but the writing is a narrative, it indicates that there is an inadequate understanding of the appropriate genre.
- Theme This criterion considers whether the writing has addressed the task or the degree to which the writing stays on task, or the inventiveness of weaving the task to produce particular effects.

- Structure   Different genres have different structural features. For example, the introduction to a description will generally classify what is being described, whereas the introduction to a narrative will generally orient the reader to the characters, time and setting of the story that will follow. There will be similar differences to other structural features of particular genres and it is important to identify these differences when assessing writing tasks.

- Rhetorical and language features   Different genres use different rhetorical strategies or figurative devices to enhance the effective-ness of the writing. In general, these types of criteria are useful indicators of a student's control of their writing or effective dis-criminators for identifying competent and/or advanced writers.

- Vocabulary   Different genres use different types of vocabulary, depending on determining categories such as topic, purpose and audience. A factual text like a science report, for example, will use a range of technical vocabulary including nominalisations and technical noun groups, whereas a literary description will use descriptive verbs, adjectives and adverbs, and affective lan-guage intended to have an emotive effect on the reader.

TEXTUAL LANGUAGE

- Connectives   Connective is a functional term for words like con-juncts and conjunctions that join linguistic units such as sentences, clauses, phrases and words in logical relationships of time, cause and effect, comparison or addition. Connectives are useful indicators of development in writing because early writers move from 'speech-like' connectives such as 'and', 'then', 'when', 'but' and so on to more complex, logical connectives that are required for the con-struction of effective complex sentences.

- Reference   Reference refers to the way in which information is introduced, maintained and expanded in a text. The use of pronouns (pronominal reference) is the most common way of maintaining reference without the clumsiness of continual naming. Control of reference is a useful indicator to assess whether students can maintain the flow of information from one sentence to the next, or successfully maintain reference to information introduced earlier it the writing

- Tense   The use of tense changes from genre to genre. Factual descriptions are generally written consistently in the present

tense, whereas narratives and arguments can move between present and past tense. In assessing student writing for appropriate use
and control of tense it is important to be aware of changes in
genre where writing may move between recounting, describing,
arguing and so on.

- Sentence structure   This criterion is a powerful indicator of
development in student writing. Writers move from simple and
compound, speech-like sentence structures to more complex,
hierarchical structures using non-finite and embedded clauses.

SYNTACTICAL LANGUAGE

Criteria in this group of categories deal with writer's competence
in control of the syntax of English sentences. It is important to assess
student writing against these criteria as they indicate many of the
basic competencies of writing that must be addressed. Criteria here
would deal with issues such as:

clause pattern	Does every statement have a subject and finite verb?
agreement	Do the auxiliaries and verb forms agree with their subjects?
verb form	Is the correct past participle of the verb used?
prepositions	Are prepositions used appropriately and correctly?
articles	Are the correct articles used?
plurals	Are plurals used correctly?
punctuation	Are sentences marked with appropriate punctuation?

SPELLING

Spelling needs to be assessed systematically and diagnostically. In
other words it is not sufficient to mark spelling for incorrectly spelt
words. Spelling should be also assessed on the level of difficulty of
the words attempted. It is best to assess 'spelling in writing' at levels
of difficulty. For example,

- high-frequency words and words with simple/common spelling
patterns: 'ai', 'ea', 'ow', or 'ay'; long vowel ending in 'e'; simple
suffixes ('ed', 'ing' or 'ly')

- less frequently used words and words with common but not simple patterns: 'wh', 'ey', 'ou', 'aw', 'ould', 'dge', 'ie', 'ough' and 'ought'; and adding suffixes to words ending in 'e', 'c' or 'l'

- words with difficult or unusual patterns: 'ible/able', 'tion', 'rh', 'ure' or 'ei'; confusion between 'l/ll', 's/ss', 'r/rr', 'ent/ant', 'ious/ous' and 'ful/full'

- challenging words appropriate to the task.

This framework for assessing writing should be used systematically with the information on assessment provided in each of the following chapters on the different genres.

CHAPTER 4

THE GENRE
OF DESCRIBING

The genre of describing is one of the fundamental functions of any language system and one of the first skills emergent language-users learn to control. It is also one of the most widely used genres across all of the learning areas, K–6 and beyond. Description enables the categorisation or classification of an almost infinite range of experiences, observations and interactions into a system that orders them for immediate and future reference, and allows us to know them either objectively or subjectively, depending on the learning area or intent of the writer. Describing is also used extensively in many text types, such as information reports, literary descriptions, descriptive recounts and, due to the need to classify and/or describe a process before explaining it, in the opening paragraphs of most explanations. Describing is also a central feature of narrative texts providing the means for developing characterisation, sense of place and key themes. Students describe when they are:

- talking or writing about a picture:

    'This is a beach. These are lots of umbrellas on it and boats on the sea.'

- writing about a character or place in a story:

  'Theo in James Valentine's book *Jump Man* is an interesting character. He has spiky hair that changes colour all the time and he wears a coat that speaks.'

- reporting on an animal:

  'A platypus is a monotreme. It has a bill and sharp claws. It lives in and near streams and isn't seen by people very often.'

While many texts, both factual and non-factual, make use of describing to differing degrees, some texts, like information reports, are predominantly about description. They formally describe phenomena from a technical point of view.

GRAMMATICAL FEATURES OF DESCRIBING

- When describing things from a technical or factual point of view, the present tense is predominantly used; for example,

  has, eats, sings, lays, swim

- Although present tense may be used in literary descriptions, it is past tense that tends to dominate; for example,

  had, was, enjoyed, seemed, sparkled

- Relational verbs are used when classifying and describing appearance/qualities and parts/functions of phenomena (is, are, has, have); for example,

  My favourite toy *is* a teddy bear because it *is* cuddly and friendly. It *is* my friend too.

  Turtles do not *have* teeth, they *have* a sharp beak instead.

  Eric the Red *is* an old man. Eric the Red *has* a greatcoat.

- Action verbs are used when describing behaviours/uses; for example,

  An ant has three body parts.
  Some ants have wings.
  The queen ant *lays* the eggs.
  Ants *live* in colonies.

- In literary and commonsense descriptions, action verbs are used metaphorically to create effect; for example,

  Mia *bubbled* with enthusiasm. Declan *smashed* the record.

- Mental verbs are used when describing feelings in literary descriptions; for example,

  She *felt* unhappy. He *liked* dancing.

- Adjectives are used to add extra information to nouns and may be technical, everyday or literary, depending on the text; for example,

Possums are *nocturnal.*	Technical
It is *grey* and *brown.*	Everyday
Her appearance was *majestic.*	Literary

Adjectives can be used on their own, as above, or as part of a noun group, as below:

Turtles are covered with a <u>hard, box-like</u> shell.	Technical
He has a <u>cool</u> hairstyle.	Everday
His <u>luminous</u>, <u>dark</u> coat gave him an <u>eerie</u> quality.	Literary

Often adjectives used in literary descriptions can be considered to be affective due to the emotive impact they have on readers. This can also be the case with the way that some verbs and adverbs are used.

- Adverbs are used to add extra information to verbs to provide more detailed description; for example,

  Turtles swim *slowly.*
  She was *always* hassling her mother.
  He could think *clearly.*

- Adverbial phrases are used in descriptions to add more information about the manner, place or time; for example,

Walruses have hair *on their lips.*	Place
The student only worked diligently *just before exams.*	Time

Literary descriptions use a range of devices to create effects such as similes, metaphors, personification and alliteration; for example,

Sally's face shone *like a beacon* when she heard that she'd won the competition.	Simile
The experience was *a nightmare* and something James would remember for the rest of his life.	Metaphor
The wind *whistled* through the trees and Harry found it difficult to sleep.	Personfication
Tired, torn and troubled, the old man stumbled through the door.	Alliteration

For more detail on how these are used in particular texts see Chapter 8 on the genre of narrating.

- Sentences and paragraphs are thematically linked to the topic of description; for example,

  The moon is a lump of rock that goes around the Earth.
  It is grey and brown.
  It is bumpy and has craters.

- Personal and literary descriptions generally deal with individual things; for example,

  my favourite toy, my house, my big bear

- Technical descriptions generally deal with classes of things, rather than individual things, for example,

  snails, turtles, volcanoes

STRUCTURE OF FORMAL DESCRIPTIONS

Formally, describing orders things into various ways of knowing them. The ordering process works in several ways; first, it generally names the thing, then it classifies it, and then it deals with its attributes, behaviours, functions and so on.

CLASSIFICATION

Language enables classification of the concrete world of experience through its ability to apply names to things. Thus the naming process is a way of taxonomising and ordering things into commonsense (everyday) or technically determined categories.

Classifications can be technical or commonsense, depending on the context within which the topic or phenomenon is being described. As a statement it locates the topic of the description into a scientifically or culturally recognised taxonomy.

The following are classifications of the same tree; one is commonsense and the other is technical. In technical descriptions the classification is formal, precise and up-front. Commonsense classifications, on the other hand, are general and rely on the everyday common understanding of readers to locate the thing being classified.

Commonsense classification	Technical classification
Tree	Kingdom: Plantae
Gum tree	Phylum: Tracheophyta
Spotted gum	Sub phylum: Pteropsida
	Class: Angiospermae
	Order: Myrtales
	Family: Myrtaceae
	Genus: Eucalyptus
	Species: maculata

Classification and description go hand in hand; we cannot describe anything unless we classify it into some sort of cultural taxonomy or framework, whether scientific/technical or commonsense/everyday.

PERSONAL AND COMMONSENSE DESCRIPTIONS

Personal descriptions are not usually as formal in their organisation as technical descriptions. A young writer's description of her toy, for example, might classify it as a particular type of toy (animal, doll or car). She may then proceed to describe its appearance and uses, but may also include a description of the writer's relationship with the toy and/or what she might do with it.

> My favourite toy is a teddy bear because it is cuddly and friendly. It is my friend too. It loves going out with me and sits on my head. One day my friend saw me out with my bear and she screamed with me.
> Year 2

The following commonsense description has been written by a Year 4 girl about one of her classmates.

Shane is a Year 4 boy. He has a cool hair style.
He is good at handball because he is tall and strong.
He likes Rugby League. He wears Reebok Pumps.
He is a sensible boy.
Year 4

LITERARY DESCRIPTIONS

This is a literary description of one of the characters from the story *The Bamboo Flute.* Note how these types of descriptions have an informal structure, although they do tend to have the classifications up-front.

Eric the Red is an old shabby man whose eyes and mouth are creased in a half-smile. His skin smells of the sun, his clothes of woodsmoke. He lives on the little red beach in the Old Garden. He doesn't speak too much but sometimes he takes out a flute from his pocket and plays beautiful notes. Eric the Red has a greatcoat, like the ones that people wear in the war, but this one is old and splodged with shades of black dye and joined together with a button and three twists of wire.
Year 6

This is also the case in the following description of Willy Wonka's chocolate factory in Roald Dahl's *Charlie and the Chocolate Factory.* Here Roald Dahl classifies the factory as first a 'chocolate' factory and 'then the largest and most famous in the world!'.

And it wasn't simply an ordinary, enormous chocolate factory either. It was the largest and most famous in the whole world! It was WONKA'S FACTORY, owned by a man called Mr Willy Wonka, the greatest inventor and maker of chocolates that there has ever been. And what a tremendous, marvellous place it was! It had huge iron gates leading into it, and a high wall surrounding it, and smoke belching from its chimneys, and strange whizzing sounds coming from deep inside it.
R. Dahl (1984) *Charlie and the Chocolate Factory*,
Harmondsworth, Puffin Books p. 16.

In William Hart-Smith's famous poem *The Beach* the metaphor of 'a quarter of golden fruit, a soft ripe melon' is used to provide a type of literary classification of the beach before engaging in an extended metaphor that comprises the remainder of the text.

The Beach

The beach is a quarter of golden fruit,
a soft, ripe melon
sliced to a half-moon curve,
having a thick green rind of jungle growth;
and the sea devours it
with its sharp,
sharp white teeth.

W. Hart-Smith (1985) *Selected poems: 1936–1984, Sydney,*
Angus and Robertson.

When characters are introduced in a novel, writers tend to provide a classification, followed by a description of the character's appearance and personality. Thus the classification acts to establish the character's role in the story, their centrality to the plot and relationship to others. This is the case below with both descriptions appearing very early in each text. It is a good idea to use extracts such as these to model to students how writers introduce characters.

Jules Santorini, about a hundred and fifty-three centimetres tall, *was a boy who felt perfectly ordinary*. He didn't think he was good looking, but he knew he wasn't ugly. His eyes seemed to be the normal distance apart. His nose appeared to be the standard model, not pointy, or snubby or flat across his face. His teeth were mainly straight but he might get braces next year. His chin has a faint cleft in it, but not enough that anyone would ever really notice. He wasn't the shortest, the fattest, the thinnest, the fastest, the slowest, the smartest, the dumbest. In fact the only area where Jules was special was in his thoughts.

J. Valentine (2002) *Time Master Jump Man*, Milsons Point, NSW, Random House, pp. 11–12.

My sister, Mrs Joe, with black hair and eyes, had such a prevailing redness of skin that I sometimes used to wonder whether it was possible she washed herself with a nutmeg-grater instead of soap. She was tall and bony, and almost always wore a coarse apron, fastened over her figure behind with two loops, and having a square impregnable bib in front, that was stuck full of pins and needles.

C. Dickens (1965) *Great Expectations*, Harmondsworth, Penguin Books, p. 40.

ANIMAL REPORTS

Many teachers of young children use animals as topics of description when teaching young writers how to write more organised descriptions. Such animal reports are somewhere in between personal descriptions and scientific reports and are an excellent way of teaching, in concrete terms, ways of formally dealing with aspects of description such as appearance and behaviour. In this example from a very early writer, you will notice that the classification comes towards the end.

The Grafe has a long tR9
it is kavod in fuRi Skin
it lodrkS Like a sPofi
thing   it eats
Leaves from trees
But it has to 90 alo9 way
down to hav a deik
it is a wild Animal

But Sumtims they
tRi to lik you

The giraffe has a long tongue.
It is covered in furry skin.
It looks like a spotty thing.
It eats leaves from trees
But it has to go a long way down
to have a drink.
The giraffe is a wild animal.
Kindergarten

The description below is based on a student's observation of ants in an ant nest. Note the ordering of the description – appearance, behaviour, habitat.

An ant is an insect.
An ant has six legs.
An ant has three body parts.
Some ants have wings.
The queen ant lays the eggs.
Ants live in colonies.
Year 1

In the following description, the young writer has attempted to order the information in the text, although inconsistencies remain. The writer has, however, managed to condense quite a lot of information into the text.

> *Frogs are amphibians*. There are over 2700 types of frogs in the world. The smallest frog is 2 cms long and the froth protects the frogs eggs.
>
> Frogs have webbed feet and slimy skin and frogs like to live in moist places. Tadpoles change into frogs when they're older. Frogs have large bulging eyes. The male can croak louder than the female. Frogs eat flies and small water insects. Frogs have long sticky tongues so they can catch small water insects and flies. Frogs have 4 legs the back legs are longer because it helps the frog jump higher.
> Year 3

INFORMATION REPORTS

Description in information reports is formalised. That is, specific aspects of the phenomenon are systematically described so that the report reflects a scientifically organised view of the world. The description stage is often divided into paragraphs which focus on specific aspects of the phenomenon being described (for example, appearance, parts, functions, behaviours, habitat).

The Moon

The moon is a lump of rock that goes around the Earth.	Classification
It is grey and brown. It is bumpy and has craters.	Appearance
It has dust and mountains. The moon does not shine, the sun does.	Properties
It is 38 000 kilometres from Earth.	Location

Year 2

Turtles

Turtles are reptiles and are cold blooded. They depend on their surroundings for their body heat.	Classification
Turtles are covered with a hard box-like shell which protects the soft body and organs. It is composed of an upper section called a carapace and a lower plate called a plaston. The head, tail and legs of turtles are covered with scales. Turtles withdraw them inside the shell for protection. Turtles have four paddle shaped flippers which help them to swim. Turtles do not have teeth, they have a sharp beak instead.	Appearance
Turtles can breathe on land and under water. They mainly eat jellyfish, sea snails and other soft-bodied, slow-moving sea animals.	Behaviours
Female turtles lay their eggs in the sand on beaches. Once the eggs are covered the female returns to the sea. When the eggs hatch the baby turtles crawl down to the sea and take care of themselves.	Reproduction

Year 6

The following is the classification paragraph from a senior secondary scientific description of possums. In italics are the classification statements, but note how the writer has broadened the framework beyond the purely scientific.

The possum is a native Australian marsupial and has been popularised as an iconic representation of Australia in cultural artifacts including children's books. *Possums are nocturnal, mainly arboreal marsupials* which occupy a niche similar to that of tree-dwelling primates of other continents; 'the upper levels of the Australian rainforest are almost exclusively the haunts of the Phalanges' (Rodríguez de la Fuente, 1974).
Year 12

THE GRAMMAR OF DESCRIBING

The following examples of student descriptions have been annotated to demonstrate some of the key grammatical features.

Relational verbs — *italics*
Action verbs — **bold**
Mental verbs — ***bold italic***
Theme — <u>underlined</u>

VERBS

This example uses the relational verb *is* for the classification and *has/have* for describing attributes. When describing behaviours, the writer has used action verbs (*lays, live*). Note that the themes of each sentence (underlined) refer directly to the topic of the description.

<u>An ant</u> *is* an insect.
<u>An ant</u> *has* six legs.
<u>An ant</u> *has* three body parts.
<u>Some ants</u> *have* wings.
<u>The queen ant</u> **lays** the eggs.
<u>Ants</u> **live** in colonies.

MY FAVOURITE TOY

The following is a commonsense description. As well as using relational verbs for the classification and appearance, the writer has used a mental verb (*loves*) to express an attitude qualifying an activity (*going out*). The themes here refer to the topic, until the last sentence where the information deals with the writer's friend and her reaction to the bear.

<u>My favourite toy</u> *is* a teddy bear because *it's* cuddly and friendly. *It's* my friend too. <u>It</u> ***loves*** **going out** with me and **sit** on my head. <u>One day my friend</u> **saw** me out with my bear and <u>she</u> **screamed** with me.

THEME

This animal report includes information about the functions of some of the turtle's attributes, and there are two action verbs in the appearance paragraph. In the first sentence of the behaviours paragraph, the writer has used the modal auxiliary (*can*), not to express probability, but to express the turtle's ability to breathe on both land and in the sea. The final paragraph functions as an explanation rather than as a description. Note the sequence of action verbs linked by temporal connectives. (See Chapter 5 for more detailed information on the grammatical features of this genre.)

> <u>Turtles</u> *are* reptiles and *are* cold blooded. <u>They</u> *depend* on their surroundings for their body heat.
> <u>Turtles</u> *have* a (hard box-like) shell which **protects** the (soft) body and organs. <u>It</u> *is* **composed** of an (upper) section *called* a carapace and a lower plate *called* a plaston. <u>The head, tail and legs of turtles</u> *have* scales for protection. <u>Turtles</u> **withdraw** them inside the shell for protection. <u>Turtles</u> have four (paddle shaped) flippers for **swim-ming**. <u>Turtles</u> *do not have* teeth, <u>they</u> *have* a (sharp) beak instead.
>
> <u>Turtles</u> can **breathe** on land and under water. <u>They</u> mainly **eat** jellyfish, sea snails and other (soft-bodied, slow-moving) sea animals.
>
> <u>Female turtles</u> **lay** their eggs in the sand on beaches. <u>Once the eggs</u> are **covered** the female **returns** to the sea. <u>When the eggs</u> **hatch** <u>the baby turtles</u> **crawl** down to the sea and **take care** of themselves.

The following text is a description of a character in a novel and, as we would expect, it is less concrete and more subjective than information and technical reports. Note the extensive use of modalities through mental verbs (*appears, seems, seems, don't seem*). You would not expect a scientific classification to start with *An ant seems to be an insect*. In a learning area like English, however, there is an extensive use of modalities from the early years on.

> <u>Ted</u> *appears to be* your average guy, he **works** for a builder, *is* some-what of a handyman and *likes* his beer.
>
> <u>However, he</u> *does have* some obvious faults. <u>He</u> *seems to stand over* his wife to the point where she **doesn't voice** her opinion on some issues. <u>Ted</u> also *seems to resent* Evie because she *is* not his own child and is **always hassling** her about **getting** a job and (petty) things that *don't seem to matter.*
> Year 9

REFERENCE

Reference, as a grammatical term, refers to the way in which estab-lished information is introduced, maintained and expanded upon in a text. The use of pronouns is a common way that reference is maintained without the clumsiness of continual naming. Pronouns only work while there is a clear line of reference to the names they are representing. Pronouns are not used indefinitely, even if there is a clear line of reference to the name; strings of pronouns make dull and uninteresting writing. Also, beginning a paragraph with a pronoun can make it difficult for readers to determine the 'who or what' to which the pronoun is referring. The following sentence refers to two things: *walruses* and *hair*. It is clear in this example that the first pronoun *they* refers to walruses because it immediately links back to *walruses*. Similarly, the second pronoun *it* refers to *hair*, and the third pronoun *they* only agrees in number with *walruses* and there can be no confusion in the reference chain. The final reference *little bit* ellipts *of hair*, although the reference is obvious.

> When <u>walruses</u> are babies <u>they</u> have a lot of <u>hair</u> but when <u>they</u> grow up <u>it</u> falls out and <u>they</u> only have a <u>little bit</u> around the upper lip.

Teaching reference chains is relatively straight forward when dealing with this genre. On the whole, the sentences are about the topic of the description and the chains of reference do not become too complex.

My Favourite Toy

My favourite toy is a teddy bear because it is cuddly and friendly. It is my friend too. It loves going out with me and sit on my head. One day my friend saw me out with my bear and she screamed with me.

Frogs

Frogs are amphibians. There are over 2700 types of frogs in the world. The smallest frog is 2 cms long and the froth protects their eggs.

Frogs have webbed feet and slimy skin and they like to live in moist places. Tadpoles change into frogs when they are older. Frogs have large bulging eyes. The male can croak louder than the female. Frogs eat flies and small water insects. Frogs have long sticky tongues so they can catch small water insects and flies. Frogs have 4 legs the back legs are longer because it helps the frog jump higher.

ADJECTIVES

Adjectives are the grammatical class that tend to carry much of the responsibility for describing. Of course all lexical items, for example, nouns, verbs, adjectives and some adverbs (as opposed to grammatical items – conjunctions, prepositions, pronouns and articles) can be used descriptively, but it is adjectives that have describing as their key function. In the text below the writer has used a range of adjectives to describe a picture of an unnamed animal. While there are a number of single adjectives, for example, *fine, peculiar, bright*, the writer has mainly used them within noun groups, for example, a *large* sack, a *long* snout, *three small* hairs.

> This animal is the size of a bear. It looks a bit like a **large** sack with hair all over it that's **fine** like grass. This monster has a **large** head with a **long** snout. Its nose is **pink** with three **small** hairs on it. Its eyes are shut because the sun is **bright**. It has its hair tied with string like a hair band. This animal has **big** shoulders and arms like a cartoon character, it has no legs. The animal's habitat is like a bunyips, **muddy** swamps and rivers. This animal is quite **peculiar**.
>
> Mitchell Year 5

Noun groups are an important grammatical resource. Teachers can use a range of activities to help students develop their competency in writing interesting and effective noun groups. For example,

- Make cards with various nouns and an article, numerative or pronoun: a cat, my dog, a monster, a picture, two statues, her friend and, in groups, have students add one or two adjectives to build noun groups. Include some technical terms and have students add appropriate adjectives. Compare and contrast the different use of this grammatical resource in technical and literary descriptions.
- Give students short texts that have a string of single adjectives or separate items of information used; for example, The boy was <u>tall</u>. He had <u>blue</u> eyes. / The bilby is a marsupial. It is <u>small</u> and lives in Australia. Have students in pairs edit these texts by condensing the information into noun groups. For example: The tall, blue-eyed boy. The bilby is a small, Australian marsupial.

For similar activities on developing noun groups in literary descriptions in particular, see the assessment strategies in Chapter 8.

TEACHING THE GENRE AND GRAMMAR OF DESCRIBING

TARGET GROUP – YEARS 1/2: CONCRETE EXPERIENCES

When introducing new knowledge throughout units of work, we should always consider the language experiences that will assist students in moving from everyday experiences/concrete knowledge to technical/abstract understanding.

- First consider the level of language development of your students. For early writers, reports on classes of animals can be too abstract. If students are first learning to write in this genre, it is better to start with a description of something that is concrete and known to them.
- Plan language activities that will bring out students' everyday/concrete knowledge. Focus questions at the beginning of a unit are a useful assessment strategy to see what and how much knowledge students are bringing to the classroom.
- As an experiential activity, take the students into the playground to observe ants. Have the students observe ants' appearance and behaviours.
- For a closer examination, have the students in groups collect ants in magnifying boxes to assist in discussion back in class.
- Conduct a brainstorming session with the class to gather information on the following aspects of ants. Record the student responses on the board.

> Appearance what do they look like?
> – black, small, six legs
>
> Behaviours what do they do?
> – crawl, run, dig, bite, move in lines

WRITING COMMONSENSE DESCRIPTIONS

Using this information, ask the students to write a short description of ants. Once this is done, write a sample of the responses on the board (expect to see a wide variation in the responses). Check to see if all texts have a classification. Discuss the effectiveness of the classification stage with the students. For example, display descriptions with and without a classification and compare and assess their effectiveness.

Ants are tiny and quick insects.
An ant is black and red.
It moves fast.
It lays eggs.
A queen ant has wings.
Ants collect food from the ground.
An ant has six legs, two antennas and three body parts.

Year 1

COMPARE AND CONTRAST CLASSIFICATIONS

Work through each of the classifications, questioning your students on the similarities and differences in the grammar. For example,

1   Ants are tiny and quick insects.
2   Ants are insects.
3   Ants are small animals.

- All are classifications but are different. Discuss the similarities and differences.

- What is common to each classification?
  - Each has the relational verb – are.
  - Each has the same subject of the sentence – Ants.

- What is different about the classifications?
  - 1 and 3 have adjectives for their object nouns (tiny and quick, small).
  - 1 and 2 use a class noun as object that is more specific as a classification statement.

Help the students to make connections between the grammar used and the purpose achieved. See this as a constructive strategy, in terms of the way that language makes meaning, rather than as a critical exercise between right and wrong.

COMPARE AND CONTRAST DESCRIPTIONS

Follow a similar procedure when you move on to a description of the appearance and behaviour. Discuss the description stage with the students.

- Pose questions such as:
  - In what way is it different from the classification?
  - What sort of things are being described?

Take some time to discuss the change in verbs; that is, the move from using relational verbs when classifying and describing appearance/attributes to using action verbs when describing behaviours.

Ask the students to identify the verbs, including those that involve an action. Look closely at the other verbs and ask the students what they are doing in the sentence; that is, the relational verbs generally function as an equal sign.

Appearance
An ant **has** three body parts.
Some ants **have** wings.

Behaviours
The queen ant **lays** the eggs.
Ants **live** in colonies.

Conduct cloze exercises, with the verbs omitted, to reinforce students' understanding of the way verbs are used differently, depending on purpose and the stage of the text.

DEVELOPING EDITING SKILLS

Consider the following commonsense description of ants and think of editing strategies for helping the students to make changes to the grammar in order to make the text more appropriate as an objective description.

Ants
An ant is an insect.
An ant can look lots of different ways.
The colours can be black, red, white and
lots more colours. An ant has anteni. I think
they have six legs. Their shiny and very tiny.
In cartoons an ant carries food but I don't
believe it. It digs a little tunnel in the ground
and builds nests.
Year 2

For instance, you would not expect an objective description to have:

- Mental verbs (think, believe), which express subjective views.
- Modalities (can look, can be), which qualify points of view.

Ask the students to think of ways of writing about the ants' vision. (*Ants have big eyes and wide vision.*)

Observation descriptions provide the same textual framework used for scientific descriptions. Your students therefore will have the writing resources necessary for the task; what is required now is an understanding of scientific classification and description.

TECHNICAL/SCIENTIFIC DESCRIPTION

Scientific description uses a particular type of classifying, taxonomising and describing the physical world. By moving from observation to scientific description you can explain how science goes about its job of organising the physical world into carefully defined frameworks or taxonomies.

Scientific description differs fundamentally from observation description, because science deals with a phenomenon as an abstract class rather than as a concrete experience. Scientific reports are not about the ants your students have observed in the playground, but about ants as a class of insect and how individual species fit into that class. Because it is an abstraction of experience, teaching scientific reports should be considered in relation to the students' cognitive development. By building up from observation description, teachers will be able to discuss how scientific classification and description differs from the types of descriptions already produced by their students. When teachers compare differences, it is important that they point out how each is performing the same task textually, but doing it from different perspectives (one is cultural, the other scientific, but both are legitimate).

Conduct activities to develop the students' relevant technical language that builds on their commonsense understanding of ants. For example:

- Ask students to label a line-drawn diagram of an ant using their commonsense language
    - head, body, legs, etc.

- Display a copy of the same diagram that uses technical language
    - thorax, abdomen, antennae, mandibles, etc.

- Compare and contrast, developing a word bank of technical terms with commonsense definitions.

- Have students write technical noun groups with these words.

The above activities focus on the appearance of ants. A similar set of activities could be used to develop the relevant technical language for behaviours.

To further develop the students' knowledge of ants, consider the following reading activities. Point out to your students the grammatical features that have already been covered in commonsense descriptions.

- Use a big book and read with the class.
- Peer reading.
- Individual reading.
- Watch a video stopping at relevant points to discuss new knowledge and/or reinforce old.

Collaborate with your librarian to conduct a research lesson in the library. You could help the students to organise this activity by providing research sheets.

RESEARCH SHEETS

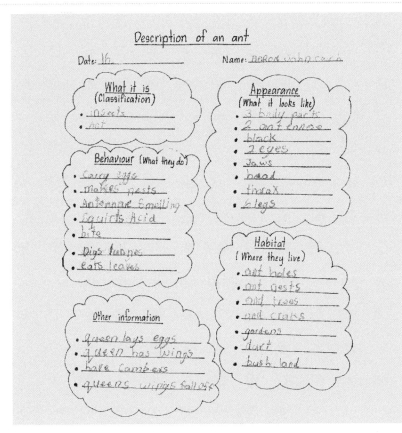

- This research activity could be done in pairs or groups.
- Point out the benefits of using an index so that the appropriate information can be found quickly.
- Show how to collect the relevant information in point form. The layout of the research sheets should help here.
- As a report-back session following the research activity, ask the students questions on each of the different categories and record their responses in point form.

Once you are satisfied that enough research has been carried out, discuss with the class the way that the information is organised and how it might be used in their report on ants.

Each information box, for example, could be used as a way of organising the text into paragraphs. Take the time to discuss any technical/scientific terms that have arisen in the research, pointing out pronunciation, spelling, scientific meaning, taxonomies and so on.

SCAFFOLDING TECHNICAL DESCRIPTIONS

Discuss how the information gathered here is similar to and different from the information in the students' experiential descriptions of ants.

Now ask the class to write their topic classifications. This could be done in research groups, pairs, or individually.

Once they are written, ask for examples to discuss with the class. In the classifications, you would be expecting some degree of technical/scientific information.

Follow a similar procedure for discussing the grammar used in the experiential descriptions (nouns, verbs, sentence structure), although as your students become more familiar with grammatical terms you can increase their competency in this area.

Make the most of this activity and the students' knowledge of the topic (ants) and of writing (generic structure and grammar), to teach them editing skills. Your role here is not to 'correct' or rewrite their work, but to ask questions that help them to make connections between the topic, the purpose, and the language features of a classification. You will find that this activity will promote enthusiastic discussion and interaction as the class becomes confident in their knowledge of how writing works. Give the class the opportunity to rewrite their classifications before moving on to the description of the ants' appearance. Again, follow a similar procedure to that used for the rest of the report, continuing to build on their knowledge of the field and the language of description.

A Description

Classification (What it is)

The ant is an insect.
It is also a social animal.

Appearance (What it looks like)

It has two antennae, six legs and
3 body parts. It's colour is black. It has
3 eyes, jaws, a head and a thorax.

Behaviour (What they do)

The ants carry eggs and make nests
They also dig tunnels. When the ant is
attacked by a human it squirts acid.
It also bites. It also smells with it's antennae.

Habitat (Where they live)

Ants live in ant holes, ant nests and
trees. They also live in cracks, gardens, dirt and bush
and

ASSESSING TEXTS USING THE GENRE OF DESCRIBING – A FACTUAL DESCRIPTION

OUTLINE OF THE TASK

The following example of an assessment task asked Year 7 students to use the information contained on a map of ancient Egypt, including its key, to write a factual description of its location, geographical features and resources. The information provided in the stimulus uses technical language such as *delta*, *wildlife* and *water source* to act as a model for the type of technical, rather than literary or commonsense, use of language required. Students were also asked to organise their work into paragraphs commencing with an introduction that is typical for this type of text. A writing task such as this can provide valuable diagnostic information of individual student's strengths and weaknesses, and indicate which teaching strategies that were used prior to completing the task require reinforcement.

ANCIENT EGYPT

The Land of Ancient Egypt

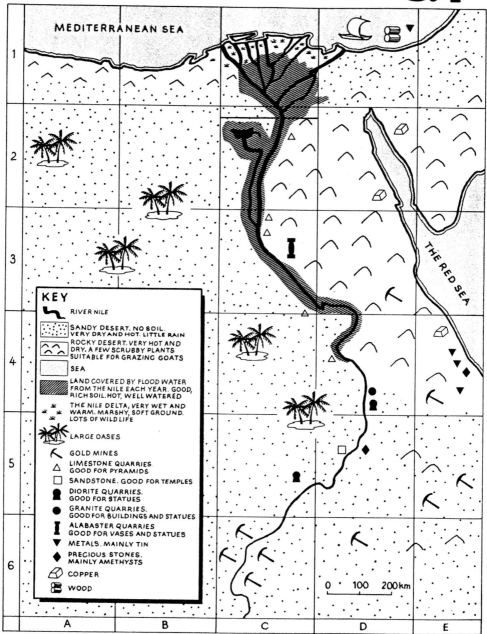

KEY

~~~ RIVER NILE

SANDY DESERT. NO SOIL. VERY DRY AND HOT. LITTLE RAIN

ROCKY DESERT. VERY HOT AND DRY. A FEW SCRUBBY PLANTS SUITABLE FOR GRAZING GOATS

SEA

LAND COVERED BY FLOOD WATER FROM THE NILE EACH YEAR. GOOD, RICH SOIL. HOT, WELL WATERED

THE NILE DELTA. VERY WET AND WARM. MARSHY, SOFT GROUND. LOTS OF WILD LIFE

LARGE OASES

GOLD MINES

LIMESTONE QUARRIES. GOOD FOR PYRAMIDS

SANDSTONE. GOOD FOR TEMPLES

DIORITE QUARRIES. GOOD FOR STATUES

GRANITE QUARRIES. GOOD FOR BUILDINGS AND STATUES

ALABASTER QUARRIES GOOD FOR VASES AND STATUES

METALS. MAINLY TIN

PRECIOUS STONES. MAINLY AMETHYSTS

COPPER

WOOD

MEDITERRANEAN SEA

THE RED SEA

0   100   200 km

The following are the assessment criteria used for assessing the task based on the appropriate generic structural and grammatical features described earlier in the chapter.

1 *Genre-based* criteria deal with the generic features of the text. This level covers the following criteria:
   - does the text describe in a technical way?
   - is the theme of the writing consistent with the task?
   - is there consistent use of third person throughout the text?
   - does the structure of the text include an introduction or classification, an elaboration of the main features of the geography, and an elaboration of the main features of the resources?
   - do the paragraphs organise the text coherently?
   - does the text contain structures which build the technical description of a report, such as noun groups and adverbial phrases?

2 *Textual Language criteria* deal with the way that the text is held together, the way that sentences are structured and how sentences work with one another. This level covers the next criteria:
   - does the text use correctly structured simple, compound and complex sentences?
   - is the text cohesive through the appropriate use of reference?
   - is the choice of tense appropriate and consistently maintained?

3 *Syntactical language* criteria deal with the internal structure of the sentences used. This level covers the next five criteria:
   - do all main clauses have essential elements such as a subject and finite verb, and do statements have the subject and finite verb in the correct order?
   - do the subject and main verb agree in person and number?
   - are prepositions used appropriately and with some variety?
   - are articles used correctly in every instance?
   - is simple and complex punctuation correct?

4 *Spelling* deals with the way that individual words are spelt.
   - are most high frequency words spelt correctly?
   - are most less frequently used words and words with common but not simple patterns spelt correctly?
   - are most words with difficult or unusual patterns spelt correctly?
   - are most challenging words appropriate to the task spelt correctly?
   - are all challenging words appropriate to the task spelt correctly?

EGYPT

1   If you went to Egypt you wouldn't get board.
    Because there are so many thing you can do.
    Like go gold mineing for a day or go and
    see wildflife at the top of river delta or
5   look precious stones. Back to gold mining from
    River Nile 200km you can go gold mining. If
    You wanted to see wildlife go the top of
    river turn to the very wet marshy soft ground
    with lots of wildlife. If you wanted to go
10 for a swim go to Red Sea or Mediterranean Sea
    or if you don't want to go for a swim go
    for a rest at the bank of the River Nile. the
    bank of the River Nile has nice soil hot well
    watered. So thats the way you would send
15 your time at Egypt.

Year 7

GENRE

GENRE AND THEME

The writing contains elements of instructing and describing, but is not generically consistent or appropriate. It reads more like a travel brochure than a factual report.

STRUCTURE

The writing is not structured appropriately for a factual report. There is no introduction/classification. The information is not organised logically, nor is it always appropriate for the required genre.

TECHNICAL LANGUAGE

The writing makes limited use of technical language. If evident it is mainly derived directly from the stimulus. Where an extended technical noun group is attempted ... *nice soil hot well watered* (l. 13–14), the syntactical structure is incorrect.

PARAGRAPHING

The writing makes no use of paragraphing

VOICE

The writing uses inappropriate use of second person throughout.

TEXTUAL LANGUAGE

SENTENCE STRUCTURE

The second sentence (l. 2) does not have a main clause. The sentences beginning (l. 3, l. 5) are structured as commands and inappropriate for the genre.

CONNECTIVES

Appropriate connectives are missing from the sentence ... *the River Nile has nice soil hot well watered* (l. 13–14).

SYNTACTICAL LANGUAGE

PREPOSITIONS

Prepositions are omitted ... *look for* (l. 5), ... *go to the top* (l. 7), or incorrect ... *at (in) Egypt* (l. 15).

ARTICLES/PLURALS

Articles are omitted ... (the) river delta (l. 4), ... (the) River Nile (l. 6), ... (the) river (l. 8), ... (the) Red Sea or (the) Mediterranean Sea (l. 10). Plural is omitted ... so many thing(s) (l. 2).

PUNCTUATION

Sentence punctuation is not always correct ... *(T)the bank of the River Nile* (l. 12–13). Incorrect capitalisation is used ... *If (y)You wanted* (l. 6–7). There is inconsistent use of apostrophes marking contractions ... *wouldn't* (l. 1), *don't* (l. 11) are used correctly ... thats l. 14 is incorrect.

SPELLING

All high frequency words and most less frequently used words are spelt correctly. There are some errors that should have been corrected through editing (l.3 *mineing* [*mining*], l. 14 *send* [*spend*]). There is also confusion with the spelling of a homophone (l.1 *board* [*bored*]).

TEACHING STRATEGIES BASED ON DIAGNOSTIC ASSESSMENT

Teaching strategies such as those described earlier in the chapter on genre, structure and technical language need to be revised explicitly with the student. In addition, the student requires some assistance in the following areas. If similar patterns emerge through the diagnostic assessment of other responses to the task, the following strategies could be incorporated into teaching programs.

DESCRIPTIVE STRUCTURES

Many students can make use of simple adjectives and couple them with a noun and also include an adverb in their writing for descriptive purposes. Others, however, have difficulty moving beyond this level of description to more complex descriptive constructions, particularly when writing technical texts where description is not necessarily foregrounded.

- To develop students' skills in writing a technical description make an OHT of a model text as below and discuss with the class.

Crocodiles

The saltwater crocodile is a large carnivorous reptile. It is found on many continents such as Australia, North and South America, Asia and Africa.

The average length of this huge reptile is approximately five metres but they can grow up to eight metres in length. The saltwater crocodile has a long lizard-like body. It has short, powerful legs and a long tail. It also has very sharp teeth and extremely powerful jaws.

In Australia crocodiles mostly live off the North Coast in warm tropical waters. Saltwater crocodiles can also be found in coastal rivers and swamps.

- Ask students:
  - what is the writer doing in this text? *describing crocodiles* what type of describing is this? *technical description*
  - where would this type of text be found? *in a science textbook or an encyclopedia*
  - what words in particular are used to describe the crocodile? Underline as they are identified/try to focus on the noun groups at first
  - What types of words are they? adjectives, for example large, carnivorous; some adverbs, for example, extremely.

- Point out how often there are two adjectives or an adjective and an adverb in noun groups to provide detailed information in a compact and efficient manner. Next underline the adverbial phrases in the passage, for example, *off the north coast, in coastal rivers and swamps* and ask students what they contribute to the description.

- After discussing the model text write a list of five items to be described on the board; for example, *kangaroos, a cyclone, the heart, gold, computers*. Ask students in pairs to write a short two- or three-sentence description using a three-word noun group and an adverbial phrase for each. Model the activity first; for example,

    Wombats are large, nocturnal marsupials. They have strong, wiry hair and a snub nose. They are found in most parts of Australia.

- Pool results identifying adjectives and adverbs in the noun groups and adverbial phrases. Follow up with an activity where students research a topic and write a description using appropriate technical vocabulary.

PREPOSITIONS

Many students encounter difficulty meeting this assessment criterion. As with other aspects of syntax and usage, NESB and ESL students tend to have particular difficulty with appropriate prepositions, as their usage is often idiomatic in nature. Improving competence in the appropriate use of prepositions is not simply a matter of enforcing formal rules such as 'Don't end a sentence with a preposition', as such rules have little relevance in contemporary English usage. Rather, provide strategies that assist students to understand how prepositions work in the context of their own writing. The following activities are useful in encouraging appropriate usage and also to acquaint students with the function of prepositions in their texts.

- First, provide students with a definition of a preposition – they are words that locate things in time and space or relate one word or phrase to another in a sentence. Brainstorm a list on the board and have students place each in a sentence. Ensure that students don't confuse prepositions with phrasal verbs; for example, in the case of *blow up, give off, turn down, face up to*. What appear to be prepositions in these examples are actually part of the verb. Pool results correcting any usage problems. Alternatively, conduct cloze exercises with selected prepositions omitted and have students fill in the blanks.

- Use lists of prepositions from Chapter 2 and brainstorm with the class for appropriate usage. Ask students to make up their own sentences using prepositions from the list.

CORRECT USE OF PLURALS AND ARTICLES

Experience demonstrates that a significant proportion of students have some difficulty with this seemingly unproblematic aspect of grammar. The plural forms of nouns in English can be irregular and hence not always apparent to many non–English-speaking background students.

- Point out that the letter 's' is the standard plural suffix, although many nouns are an exception to this rule. Nouns ending in *s*, *z*, *tch*, *dg*, *sh* take the plural form of *es*. Nouns ending in a *consonant + y* change the *y* to *i* and add *es*. There are a group of old words that change their vowels to show the plural: *man–men*, *woman–women*, *tooth–teeth*, *foot–feet*, *mouse–mice* and so on. Finally, there are a group of words that have the same form for singular and plural such as *sheep*, *fish*, *deer*, *series*, *species* and so on.

- For an individual activity, present students with a list of nouns from the above groups. Have students write the appropriate plural forms for each noun.

- Articles are the most common words we use in writing; it is hard to write a sentence without using one or two of them. When reference is made to people or things as generic classes, either the definite or indefinite articles can be used for the singular and no article should be used for the plural. When no article is used it is called a *zero article*.

    The frog is an amphibian.
    A frog is an amphibian.
    Frogs are amphibians.

- For an individual activity, present students with a list of sentences with the articles missing. Have students insert the appropriate articles and identify whether they are definite or indefinite.

After completing these activities have students complete another assessment task to write a factual description and compare results with the first task.

CHAPTER 5

THE GENRE
OF EXPLAINING

The genre of explaining is a fundamental language function for understanding the world and how it operates. The process of explaining is used to logically sequence the way that we and our environment physically function, as well as understanding and interpreting why cultural and intellectual ideas and concepts prevail.

Consequently, explaining is a language process that young children are exposed to from an early age. Consider the following instruction to a young child.

> No you can't go on the road, Darling, because there's a lot of cars using the road and they travel very fast and they cannot see little children and if they hit you they could hurt you very badly.

The parent in this case is offering the child more than a bald instruction. The instruction *No you can't go on the road, Darling*, is followed with a quite complex causal explanation that incorporates five action verbs – *using, travel, see, hit, hurt*.

Children can ask devastatingly simple questions that defy a simple explanation. For example,

Why doesn't that big boat sink?
How does the wind get made?

Parents become adept at providing simple answers that generally satisfy a young child's thirst for knowledge. The act of explaining, however, remains one of the fundamental language processes in providing learners with new understandings of the world and how it operates.

For teachers, explaining is a frequently used spoken genre. For students it is an essential genre for accumulating knowledge about the world, demonstrating that knowledge, and developing a capacity to question and critically assess information. It is clearly, therefore, a generic process integral to learning and, not surprisingly, it is constantly used across all learning areas, from infants to the senior secondary years.

Explaining has two main orientations – to explain *why* and to explain *how*; often both will appear in an explanatory text.

Explaining how
When Beryl the lollypop lady sees children who want to cross the road, she holds up her STOP sign and then walks to the middle of the crossing and stands there until all the children have crossed.

Explaining why
Beryl is a lollypop lady who stops the traffic when children want to cross. When drivers see Beryl with the STOP sign, they know they must stop and allow the children to cross.

Explaining how and why
When children want to cross the road, the lollypop lady holds up her STOP sign and drivers know that they must stop and allow the children to cross.

EARLY EXPLANATIONS

In the early years of school, students will generally use the process of explaining to talk and write about personal experiences and concrete knowledge. As well, they will be frequently exposed to explanations from the teacher about a wide range of phenomena and experiences. In the primary years, explaining is used across the curriculum, however, it tends to be predominant as written texts in science, technology and social science subjects.

As students develop both cognitively and in their use of oral language, they can move towards the process of writing explanations in a range of learning contexts. From a teaching point of view, this movement needs to be structured developmentally. What needs to be understood, however, is that explanations are generally 'dense' texts; that is, they condense a lot of information into brief explanatory sequences. Students can therefore find writing explanations quite difficult if they do not have a comprehensive understanding of the way to order and sequence the relevant processes (verbs) that comprise the explanation.

GRAMMATICAL FEATURES OF EXPLAINING

- Explanations are often about particular processes involving classes of things, which means that the nouns are general rather than specific. For example,

  germination, cars, cities, schools

- Explanations about classes of things use verbs in the present tense unless, of course, the class of things no longer exists – dinosaurs, for example.

- Explanations that deal with specific things such as particular events or concepts, on the other hand, can be in the present, past or future tense. For example,

  This *is* my plan for a house. It *will* be a two-storey house so you *will* see the view.

- Processes or verbs are used in explanations where one process or verb is linked to another process or verb in such a way that a logical sequence is produced. In the example below, the verbs (*italic*) are sequenced temporally and causally.

  When the fuel *burns* it *expands* with great force. The exhaust from the burning fuel, however, *can only escape* through the exhaust nozzle at the tail of the rocket. This *creates* a thrust which *forces* the rocket forward.

- In commonsense and technical explanations action verbs are mainly used, for example, *burns, expands, forces,* whereas in interpretative explanations mental verbs may be used, for example, *suggest, reflects.*

- Explanations generally require connectives – words that join the verbs together so that they logically indicate sequences that are temporal – *when, then, first, after this.*

  or causal, for example, *because, so.*

- While more a feature of some forms of instructing and arguing, explanations will sometimes make use of modality. For example,

  Workers use bulldozers or picks and shovels to clear recent rubbish from the site. When they reach levels where relics *might* be found the work is much slower.

- Pronominal reference is also an important feature of explanations. The use of pronouns helps to maintain the thematic cohesion of the text. The type of pronouns used are either personal pronouns, in **bold** or demonstrative, <u>underlined</u>.

  When the Earth orbits around the sun **it** is tilted on an axis. Because of <u>this</u> the Earth is in different positions during the year.

  The Hubble Telescope can see seven times further into the Universe than it would from Earth. When the light rays hit the main mirror, light detectors change **them** into television signals. <u>These</u> signals are then sent to a radio dish somewhere on Earth.

STRUCTURE OF EXPLANATIONS

As we have seen, explaining deals with the processes involved in understanding and making explicit the how and/or why of particular phenomena, events and concepts. A structural and grammatical framework for teaching this genre is a useful way for teachers to move students towards competence in performing this essential learning process.

PERSONAL AND COMMONSENSE EXPLANATIONS

As in the case of personal descriptions, personal and commonsense explanations are not usually as formal in their organisation as scientific or technical explanations. However, in regard to structure, the first thing most explanations do is to classify and describe the phenomenon, event, or concept. The reader of an explanation generally needs to know what it is that is about to be explained. For example,

This picture *is* my new truck. It *has* red wheels and a man driving.	Description

First it has to *go* at the top of the slide and when you *push* the button it *goes* down and around.	Explanatory sequence

Sophie, Year 2

In this example we can see that Sophie has begun her piece of writing with a description of the truck she has drawn. She then proceeds to explain how the truck works. This constitutes the second structural feature of an explanation – the explanatory sequence. Explanatory sequences are made up of processes/verbs arranged in a logical order that tell how, why and, as we have seen, often how and why combined. Sophie has arranged the verbs as follows:

it *goes* at the top
you *push* the button
it *goes* down and around.

As readers, we have a clear idea from the explanation about how the truck works.

The Water Cycle

Rain comes from clouds. It helps us to stay alive. Animals and plants need rain.	Description stage

When rain falls it goes into the ground and rivers. Then it goes into plants and animals drink it. The rivers go into the sea and the sun makes the rain go back to the clouds.	Explanatory sequence

I like the rain. Rain is good for you.	Evaluation interpretation

In the example shown above there is a slight difference in the way this student has organised their text. Their opening paragraph is not so much a classification/description, it is an introduction which provides some information about one aspect of the process about to be explained. The student has followed this with an explanatory sequence on how the water cycle works.

You will notice that following the explanatory sequence, the student has moved into a personal observation and judgement to complete the text. This kind of comment often appears in young writers' texts, but it is neither necessary nor appropriate in a technical explanation.

SCIENTIFIC/TECHNICAL EXPLANATIONS

Scientific and technical explanations are text types frequently used to induct students into the learning areas of science and technology, and mathematics. The genre of explaining is a fundamental process in the exchange of information and ideas in these learning areas.

While students frequently encounter this genre in both books and in the way that information is orally presented, they should also be learning to write formal technical and scientific explanations, because:

- they develop the skills of logically organising scientific and technical knowledge into explanatory sequences using the appropriate technical language; and

- as they move towards competence in constructing formal scientific and technical explanations and using appropriate technical terminology, they will become more confident participants in the scientific and technical subject areas.

We have already seen that explanations generally begin with an introductory paragraph that often includes a classification and description and this is then followed by an explanatory sequence. The next example demonstrates the role these features play in the explanation of scientific phenomena.

Flotation

Flotation is a technical term that deals with the degree objects stay on the surface or sink in liquids. Objects that float are said to be buoyant.	Description stage

> When a solid object is placed in a liquid it is forced up by the density of the liquid. If the density of the solid is greater than the density of the liquid then the solid will sink. If the density of the solid is less than the density of the liquid then the object will float. That is why objects water and why heavy objects like rocks will sink.
>
> Causal explanatory sequence

In scientific and technical explanations, the introductory paragraph generally has the function of classifying and describing the particular phenomenon to be explained.

- It classifies the phenomenon or concept as a part of a particular group of things; for example,

    Flotation is a technical term ...

- It describes the phenomenon or concept in relation to other things within the same network; for example,

    Objects that float are said to be buoyant.

- It describes essential features or uses that are relevant to the subsequent explanatory sequence; for example,

    ... a technical term that deals with the degree objects stay on the surface or sink in liquids. Objects that float are said to be buoyant.

Once the phenomenon or concept has been located in this scientific frame, the explanation moves into the explanatory sequence stage. This involves the sequencing of verbs arranged either temporally or causally, or in combinations of these; for example,

    is placed ... forced ... sink ... float ...

Explanatory sequences in general follow a pattern of two or three verbs, followed by a brief description/evaluation, followed by another sequence of verbs, and so on. This is clearly evident in the lengthy explanation on bees shown overleaf.

The Life-Cycle of Bees

Bees are social insects that live in large groups called colonies. Of all the insects, only bees, ants, wasps and termites take care of their families. All bees in a colony have special jobs and social responsibilities. Colonies of bees live in well-organised places called hives. There are three types of bees in a colony: a queen, the female workers and the male drones. The queen bee produces eggs which are cared for by the female worker bees. In a hive there are thousands of worker bees, a few dozen drones and only one queen. The male drones have only one job in a hive – to mate with the queen.	Description stage
When a new queen hatches from her queen cell, she must mate with a drone who provides millions of tiny sperm cells that the queen bee stores in a special pouch in her body. Just before she lays new eggs, she fertilises each one with a sperm cell, so that it can develop into a new worker.	Sequenced explanation (mating)
The egg laid by the queen is so small that it is barely visible. Three days after it is laid it hatches into a white larva. A few minutes after the larva has hatched, a worker appears at the cell to feed it a special food called 'royal jelly'. This feeding process goes on continuously. About once a minute a worker arrives to feed the larva. For the first two days the larva is fed royal jelly and the following four days it is fed 'bee bread' – a mixture of flower pollen and honey. Over this period the larva grows so quickly, it fills the entire cell.	Sequenced explanation (larva)
It now begins to produce a sticky silk from glands near its mouth. Weaving back and forth, it spins the silk into a lacy cocoon. At this stage the workers stop feeding the larva and seal the cell with wax. Inside the cocoon, the soft, legless body of the grub stiffens. Outlines of legs, wings, eyes, antennae, begin to form. The larva is changing into a pupa.	Sequenced explanation (incubation and pupa)
Twelve days later, a sharp new pair of jaws begins to cut away at the wax sealing the cell. The cell opens and the new worker bee appears. After about one day, this new bee is busy at work in the organisation of the hive.	Sequenced explanation (emergence from cocoon)

INTERPRETATIVE EXPLANATIONS

Explaining is also a key generic resource used in interpreting phenomena. These types of texts tend to be used predominantly in English and the Creative Arts, and while they can appear as singularly generic texts, the process of explaining in this way is also evident in a range of multi-generic texts such as reviews and personal responses. Interpretative explanations are closely allied with the genre of arguing in that much of the elaboration of a proposition is explanation. Interpretative explanations are quite sophisticated texts. The kind of personal responses that younger writers produce tend to be more like 'proto arguments' comprising an opinion or point and then a simple causal explanation; for example, *I don't think Mr Twit is nice because he does nasty things* and *I don't like it because it is scary*. The actual movement beyond this to a more complex explanation is more evident in students' writing in the later years of primary and at the beginning of high school.

Interpretative explanations have some structural similarities with the other types of explanations already discussed. They will generally commence with an introductory paragraph that is then followed with an explanation. Where these types of explanations differ, however, is that the explanation is primarily causal and the focus is interpretation. This is the case in the text below, which is an interpretation of an artwork. The text commences with a description of the painting, followed by an explanation of how the artist has achieved particular effects through the manipulation of different visual elements.

Powerhouse 3 *is* a powerful painting that *depicts* Mary Martin's view of an industrial landscape.

Martin *manipulates* the visual elements of colour, shape, texture, tone and composition *to project* her rather bleak view of industry.

She *uses* colours such as dark blues, greys and red *to suggest* the effects of pollution. While these colours *dominate* the work, she also *uses* yellow and orange *to symbolise* the heat and energy of molten metal.

Martin *presents* the scene as a series of monumental block-like structures which *reflect* the dominance of industry over nature. This use of hard-edged three-dimensional forms further *emphasises* the destructive nature of industry that seemingly *cannot be changed* or *improved*.

THE GRAMMAR OF EXPLAINING

COMMONSENSE EXPLANATIONS

Explanations that deal with things from an everyday point of view are generally loosely structured and are recognisable by the way that they can move from one thing to another unproblematically. Their grammar, however, is fairly stable; here we find sequences of processes represented by action verbs and connected by temporal and causal connectives.

> **How Birds Make Their Nests**
> Birds find lots of things to make their nests.
> They find twigs and leaves and straw. They weave it
> around a branch of a tree. Then they have their
> babies and find worms for them.
> *Lucia, 6*

In this example, Lucia competently arranges the sequence of processes or actions birds perform in order to build a nest and feed their young into a single explanatory sequence using the following action verbs:

> find, weave, have (babies), find

To some extent the placement of the verbs has established the temporal sequence but this is reinforced by the use of the temporal connective *then*.

TECHNICAL EXPLANATIONS

We have seen that in scientific and technical explanations, the introduction generally has the function of classifying and describing the particular phenomenon to be explained.

> **Television Cameras**
> *The television camera is a complex piece of photographic*

machinery that converts images into picture signals. It is a key element in the process of communicating pictures and sound through the air via radio waves, known as television.

The light reflected from an image in front of the camera passes through the camera lens. The light is then focused onto a special computer chip called a CCD or charge coupled device.

The CCD converts the light into electricity. Bright areas of the image create more electricity than dark areas and so the image becomes a collection of bright and dark areas which the camera then breaks down into small parts and reads as separate bits of information.

In performing the function of classifying the television camera as a member of a particular group of things, the description stage uses a relational verb *is* in a clause structure that can be represented as *x is y* or $x = y$:

A television camera is a complex piece of machinery …

In describing the television camera in relation to other elements within the same network of phenomena, the relational verb *is* is again used; for example,

It is a key element …

As we have seen before, when an explanation moves into the explanatory sequence stage the grammar changes significantly. In this case the sequence is made up of a series of action verbs:

Reflected… passes … focuses onto … converts …
… create … becomes … breaks down … reads …

These are joined in temporal and causal relationships by temporal, causal and additive connectives:

then, so, then, and, then, and, so that.

The Life Cycle of Coral
Corals **reproduce** by the spawning process. Eggs and sperm join together in the water **to form** planulae. The planulae *then* drifts in the ocean as plankton for about a month. *However*, most of their lives they **are threatened** by their predator, the Whale Shark. Whale

Sharks **are attracted** to the plankton and then **eat** them. *When* the planulae finally **settles**, it **turns** into a coral polyp.

Mitchell Year 6

A similar use of grammar is evident in the text above. In the introduction to his explanation this writer has stated the process to be explained. In the following explanatory sequence he has used a series of action verbs to outline the life cycle of coral:

join, to form, drifts, are threatened, are attracted, eat, settles, turns

The mainly temporal sequencing of the text is reinforced by the use of *then* and *when* with a causal relationship marked by the use of the connective, *however*.

INTERPRETATIVE EXPLANATIONS

While there are some clear links between the grammar of commonsense, technical and interpretative explanations, where the latter differs is in the emphasis these types of explanatory texts place on establishing causal relationships and their use of mental verbs. In the text below the relational verb *is* is used in introducing and providing a summary description of the artwork. In the explanation which follows in the remaining three paragraphs there is a clear causal relationship established between the action verbs (manipulates, uses, uses, dominates, presents, cannot be changed, improved) and the mental verbs (to project, to suggest, to symbolise, reflect, emphasises).

Powerhouse 3 *is* a powerful painting that *depicts* Mary Martin's view of an industrial landscape.

Martin *manipulates* the visual elements of colour, shape, texture, tone and composition *to project* her rather bleak view of industry.

She *uses* colours such as dark blues, greys and red *to suggest* the effects of pollution. While these colours *dominate* the work, she also *uses* yellow and orange *to symbolise* the heat and energy of molten metal.

Martin *presents* the scene as a series of monumental block-like structures which *reflect* the dominance of industry over nature. This use of hard-edged three-dimensional forms further *emphasises* the destructive nature of industry that seemingly *cannot be changed* or *improved*.

TEACHING THE GENRE OF EXPLAINING

TARGET GROUP: YEARS 3/4

The following teaching ideas are drawn from a unit about space. The focus here is the effects of the Sun on the Earth, content that links nicely with an examination of the genre of explaining. While the emphasis is on examining this genre some reference is also made to describing. In planning a unit of work it would be necessary to first revise aspects of the genre of describing by broadening the investigation of space to include work on different features of the solar system and the universe. The class could:

- address an intergalactic postcard which includes their name, street, town/suburb, state, country, planet, planetary system, galaxy and conclude with 'the universe'

- use this activity for a brainstorming session about features of the universe

- make a class model of the solar system

- read and discuss information books about the planets in the solar system focusing on the structure and grammar of the language used to describe each

- conduct group-based research on a particular planet and have each group report their findings to the class in the form of an information report.

This process of structuring a unit, by first describing and then explaining, is an effective way of scaffolding students' learning. It is particularly valuable in science where students are required to perceive the world, not merely in terms of an observation of concrete phenomena, but as an abstraction of experience; that is, the discipline of science names and codes the world within a particular system of meaning generally far removed from students' own immediate understanding of the world. The genres of describing and explaining assist students' induction into the 'world' of space by making connections between the content and the language required to process this body of knowledge.

CONCRETE EXPERIENCES

Ask the class what they think are the effects of the Sun on the Earth. Conduct a general discussion about day and night and the seasons.

Using a globe or a ball to represent the Earth and a torch to represent the Sun, demonstrate to the class how day and night occur. If using a globe, point out specific countries and pose questions such as – 'If it is night in Australia which part of the world is in daylight?'

During the demonstration explain the following:

> A day is the amount of time a planet takes to complete a full rotation. The Earth's day is 24 hours long. Day and night are formed as the Earth rotates on its axis around the Sun. When the Sun's rays hit the area of the Earth that is facing it, this area is experiencing day. The area that is not facing the Sun is in darkness and is experiencing night.

Have students bring in a torch and basketball from home and conduct the same activity in groups, so that they gain a more immediate experience of this concrete representation of how day and night occur.

ANALYSING EXPLANATIONS

STRUCTURE

Following these activities, jointly construct an explanation with the class on the board, using the above text as a guide. Alternatively, make an overhead of the explanation provided above and discuss. When this is completed begin to analyse the text with the class. Ask students what the text is doing.

Point out that in this text there is a mixture of describing and explaining. Clarify this point by examining whether a sentence, or part of a sentence, is about *what*, and is therefore describing, or *how* and/or **why**, and so explaining, as is indicated below.

A day is the amount of time a planet takes to complete a full rotation. The Earth's day is 24 hours long.	Describing

Day and night are formed as the Earth rotates on its axis around the Sun. When the Sun's rays hit the area of the Earth, that is facing it, this area is experiencing day. The area that is not facing the Sun is in darkness and is experiencing night.	Explaining

Point out that while this type of text could be called an explanation, as this is its overall purpose, it both describes what, and explains how and why, in the one text. This is often the case with explanations that will generally start with a classification/description of a phenomenon before a process is explained. The length of the explanatory sequence depends on the process being explained. In the explanation of day and night, describing is used to provide a classification of a day in general, and the length of a day on Earth. This is followed by a short explanation of how day and night are formed.

GRAMMAR

VERBS

- Begin to focus on the language features of the explanation, particularly those that signal whether the language is describing or explaining.

- Ask students what language features suggest that the first two sentences are classifying or describing – the use of the relational verb *is*.

- Identify the verbs in the remainder of the passage (underline each on the board) and ask students what type of verbs occur when the text is explaining – action verbs.

are formed
rotates
hit
is facing
is not facing
is experiencing

- Ensure students are clear about *is* used as an auxiliary in an action verb group, and *is* used as a relational verb, as in, the opening paragraph. To clarify these points have students complete exercises where they distinguish between these different uses of *is*. These could either be prepared by the teacher, or students could write 10 sentences with five examples of each use; that is, relational verb or auxiliary.

- Return to the discussion about action verbs. Consider why they would be used in an explanatory sequence. Explain how a process is a series of actions. Refer to the action verbs underlined on the board and ask students if they can identify any connection between them; that is, could these verbs be placed in any order, or, are they arranged in a particular sequence?

- Discuss how there is a general sequence to the verbs. Each verb represents a stage in the process. The process of how day and night are formed would be confused if the order of verbs were changed.

- Spend time practising identifying action verbs in short explanatory sequences using extracts from texts such as those below.

Why do orbits work?

An orbit works like an object being spun around on a piece of string. Because of the force of us spinning the string, it pushes the object out. However, the string stops the object from flying away because it holds it back. The two forces, one pulling and one pushing, make the stone go around in a circle.

1	works
2	being spun
3	spinning
4	pushes
5	stops
6	flying
7	holds
8	pulling
9	pushing
10	make
11	go

How do satellites stay up in the sky?
The earth's gravity works like the string. When a satellite is launched, the force of the rocket pushes it away from the earth. The earth's gravity then pulls it back and creates a tension like the string. These two forces make the satellite stay in orbit.

1 works
2 is launched
3 pushes
4 pulls
5 creates
6 make
7 stay

How do rockets work?
Rockets work like balloons. When rockets are fired, they burn vast quantities of fuel. The exhaust gases created by the burning fuel are then forced out of the nozzle at the end of the rocket, which push-es the rocket forward.

1 work
2 are fired
3 burn
4 created
5 are forced
6 pushes

On completing this task, discuss students' responses pointing out the sequential nature of action verbs in explanations.

CONNECTIVES

- Following this, return to the explanation on the board or OHT. Ask the class:

  - is there any other word which indicates that the text is explaining rather than describing? – 'when'
  - what type of word is it? – a connective
  - what type of connective is it? – a temporal or time connective

- Point out how a sequence is reinforced by using connectives. Ask students for other examples of temporal or time connectives, such as *when, after, before, next* and *then*, and compile a list on the board.

- Explain how explanations also use causal connectives to establish relationships between processes such as *because, as a result* and *therefore*. Compile another list of these words on the board.

- To further examine the use of connectives in explanations, distribute texts to students, such as those below, and in groups have them identify the connectives and indicate whether they are temporal or causal. Discuss students' results.

Why do orbits work?

An orbit works like an object being spun around on a piece of string. Because of the force of us spinning the string, it pushes the object out. However, the string stops the object from flying away because it holds it back. The two forces, one pulling and one pushing, make the stone go around in a circle.

1	because	Causal
2	however	Causal
3	because	Causal

How do satellites stay up in the sky?

The earth's gravity works like the string. When a satellite is launched, the force of the rocket pushes it away from the earth. The earth's gravity then pulls it back and creates a tension like the string. These two forces make the satellite stay in orbit.

1	when	Temporal
2	then	Temporal

How do rockets work?

Rockets work like balloons. When rockets are fired, they burn vast quantities of fuel. The exhaust gases created by the burning fuel are then forced out of the nozzle at the end of the rocket, which pushes the rocket forward.

1	When	Temporal
2	then	Temporal

SCAFFOLDING EXPLANATIONS

- Move onto an examination of how seasons occur. Point out how this is another way the Sun affects the Earth.

- Using a globe of the Earth point out the following features:
  - the Equator
  - the northern and southern hemispheres
  - the Tropic of Capricorn and Tropic of Cancer
  - the North and South Poles
  - the axial inclination (23.44 degrees).

- Have students label their own diagram of the Earth with these features.

- To demonstrate how the seasons occur, once again take a globe of the Earth and a ball to represent the Sun. Place the ball, or 'Sun', in a container on a desk and move the globe, at desk height, around the ball while spinning it around and simulating the tilt of the axis. Point out the four key dates in the year that signal the start of a new season. Also indicate the position of the Sun, in relation to the equator and the two tropics, at these times.

- Indicate the different seasons in the northern and southern hemispheres. To ensure the class understands the process ask for volunteers to demonstrate the position of the Earth in relation to the Sun for the northern summer, southern summer, northern and southern winters, and spring and autumn in both hemispheres.

- After conducting this activity draw a diagram of how the seasons occur on the board and discuss with the class. Alternatively, display the diagram shown below. Ask students if this is an accurate representation of the process that was modelled in class.

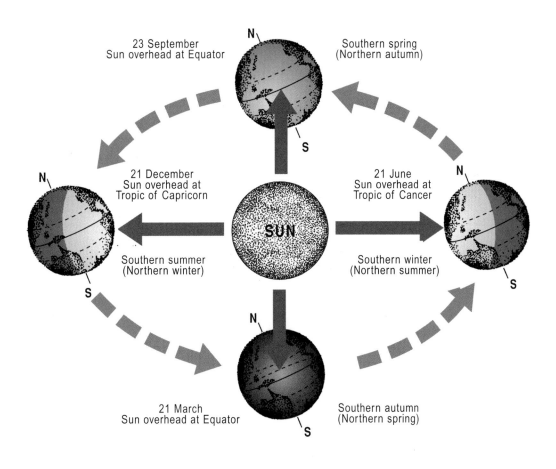

- Use this diagram as a stimulus for students to write their own draft explanation on how the seasons occur. Before students begin, distribute the scaffold, shown below, and discuss the different stages with the class. Point out how they need to describe what the seasons are in their first paragraph. In the second paragraph, they are to explain how spring and autumn occur, and in the third paragraph how summer and winter occur. Remind students about the grammar of explaining and how they can focus on linking verbs and connectives to establish an explanatory sequence.

Explanation of how seasons occur

Classification of seasons	
Explanatory sequence of spring and autumn	
Explanatory sequence of summer and winter	

COMPARING AND CONTRASTING STUDENTS' TEXTS

- Select two or three students' texts to discuss with the class. An example is provided below.

The Seasons

During the year the Earth has four seasons spring, summer, autumn and winter. A year is approximately 365 days in length. This is the amount of time the Earth takes to complete its orbit around the Sun.

When the Earth orbits around the Sun it is tilted on an axis. Because of this the Earth is in different positions during the year. On the 21st of March and the 23rd of September the Sun's rays shine straight down on the Equator. On these days the length of day and night are equal everywhere. When the Earth is in this position the seasons are autumn and spring. Autumn starts in the southern hemisphere on the 21st of March and spring starts in the northern hemisphere on the same day. Accordingly, the seasons are reversed in the hemispheres on the 23rd of September.

On the 21st of June the Sun is overhead at the Tropic of Cancer. This means the northern hemisphere is experiencing summer and the southern hemisphere winter. On the 21st of December the Sun is overhead at the Tropic of Capricorn and so the southern hemisphere is experiencing summer and the northern hemisphere is in winter.

- Start to examine the language used in the texts. Ask students:
  - what is the overall purpose of the text?
  - what is the language doing in the first paragraph?
  - does the text start with a description?
  - what signals the beginning of the explanation?
  - does describing also appear at intervals in the explanatory sequence?
  - why does this happen?

- Have students use the class discussion of these texts to inform an edit and redraft of their own work. Ensure they consider the structure and grammar of their own texts and that they distribute to peers for additional advice.

ASSESSING TEXTS USING THE GENRE OF EXPLAINING

OUTLINE OF THE TASK

The following example of an assessment task asked Year 7 students to use the information in a diagram of the processes that make up paper recycling. The information provided in the stimulus uses technical language such as *paper collection*, *non-paper removal* and *paper pulping* to act as a model for the type of technical, rather than literary or commonsense, use of language required. Students were also asked to organise their work into paragraphs commencing with an introduction that is typical for this type of text. A writing task such as this can provide valuable diagnostic information of individual student's strengths and weaknesses, and indicate which teaching strategies that were used prior to undertaking the task require reinforcement. For this task they were told to organise their work into paragraphs, starting with a paragraph that introduces the explanation. They were told to use well-structured sentences that make sense and to pay attention to spelling and punctuation.

They were also given the following stimulus:

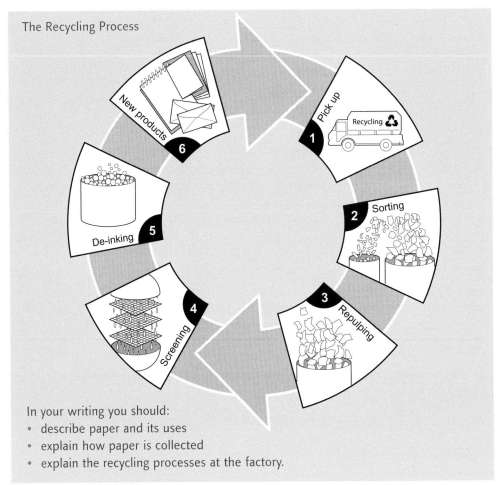

The Recycling Process

1 Pick up — Recycling

2 Sorting

3 Repulping

4 Screening

5 De-inking

6 New products

In your writing you should:
• describe paper and its uses
• explain how paper is collected
• explain the recycling processes at the factory.

The following are the assessment criteria used for assessing the task based on the appropriate generic structural and grammatical features described earlier in the chapter. Some of these criteria are similar to those used for the task on writing a factual description such as syntactical language and spelling, while the genre-based and textual language criteria will vary.

1 *Genre-based* criteria deal with the generic features of the text. This level covers the following criteria:
   - does the writing explain?
   - is the theme of the writing consistent with the task?
   - is third person used consistently throughout the text?
   - is the structure of the writing consistent with the genre?
   - does the text contain structures which build the technical aspects of the explanation?

2 *Textual language criteria* deal with the way that the text is held together, the way that sentences are structured and how sentences work with one another. This level covers the next three criteria:
   - does the text use correctly structured simple, compound and complex sentences?
   - is the text cohesive through the appropriate use of reference?
   - is the choice of tense appropriate and consistently maintained?

3 *Syntactical language* criteria deal with the internal structure of the sentences used. This level covers the next five criteria:
   - do all main clauses have essential elements such as a subject and finite verb, and do statements have the subject and finite verb in the correct order?
   - do the subject and main verb agree in person and number?
   - are prepositions used appropriately and with some variety?
   - are articles used correctly in every instance?
   - is simple and complex punctuation correct?

4 *Spelling* deals with the way that individual words are spelt.
   - are most high-frequency words spelt correctly?
   - are most less-frequently used words and words with common but not simple patterns spelt correctly?
   - are most words with difficult or unusual patterns spelt correctly?
   - are most challenging words appropriate to the task spelt correctly?
   - are all challenging words appropriate to the task spelt correctly?

Paper Recycling

1 Paper is recycled by machines.
You throw out papers and cardboard packages or any thin
to do with paper, then a truck comes and
collects it. And take it to a place where

5   paper is recycled.
This is how it works. first it goes
in a machine and it sorts out anything not
made of paper.
After that all the other materials like plastic,
10 glass, aluminium cans etc. must also be recycled.
Now after all of that it is ready
to go in the truck and be re-used.
That is the way how paper recycled.

Year 8

As has been described above, this genre is used across a range of Key Learning Areas and there may be subtle changes both structurally and grammatically to the genre when explaining different types of phenomena. Explanations of 'how' are generally the most simple structurally and grammatically, and for this reason they are useful as assessment tasks when wanting to diagnostically assess student competence in this genre.

GENRE

GENRE AND THEME

The writing explains each aspect of the process of paper recycling and the theme addresses the task; for example, the topic of the explanation is the subject of most sentences.

STRUCTURE

The text begins with an inappropriate introduction for an explanation. This is followed by an appropriate series of explanatory sequences, but the text concludes ineffectively.

IMPERSONAL VOICE

The writing mostly uses impersonal and objective language; however, the introduction slips into second person (l. 2).

PARAGRAPHING

The text is not organised into paragraphs − every sentence begins on a new line.

TEXTUAL LANGUAGE

SENTENCE STRUCTURE

The writing uses a range of simple and compound sentences. However, the sentences from lines 3 to 5 are inappropriately structured; that is, *You throw out papers and cardboard packages or any thin to do with paper. <u>Then</u> a truck comes and collects it <u>and take</u> it to a place where paper is recycled.*

CONNECTIVES

There is a varied use of appropriate connectives for an explanation of 'how' (l. 3 *then*, l. 4 and l. 7 *and*, l. 6 *first*, l. 9 *after that*, l. 10 *now after all of that*).

TENSE

Tense is consistently and appropriately maintained throughout the text.

SYNTACTICAL LANGUAGE

CLAUSE PATTERN

Most main clauses have a subject and finite verb; however, the final clause does not have a finite verb, l. 14 *how paper (is) recycled.*

AGREEMENT

Incorrect verb form (l. 4) for third personal singular subject, *And take(s) it to a place.*

PREPOSITIONS

There is some variety in prepositions, l. 1 *by*, l. 3 *with*, l. 4 *to*, l. 7 *in* and so on.

ARTICLES/PLURALS

All articles and plurals are correct.

PUNCTUATION

The second sentence l. 6 does not begin with a capital letter.

SPELLING

All high-frequency words and most less frequently used words are spelt correctly, l. 1 *machines*, l. 2 *cardboard*, l. 4 *collects*, l. 7 *machine*, l. 9 *materials*, l. 10 *aluminium*.

SUMMARY

This text demonstrates an emerging control of writing a technical explanation based on visual stimulus. The writing has the basic structure for an explanation and there are attempts to use some technical language. The writer is generally able to construct effective simple and compound sentences that sequence information. The text demonstrates satisfactory control of a range of simple spelling and punctuation, including some complex and technical vocabulary. However, work needs to be undertaken on developing consistent use of voice appropriate to the demands of this type of writing.

TEACHING STRATEGIES BASED ON DIAGNOSTIC ASSESSMENT

Teaching strategies similar to those described earlier in this chapter on genre, structure and technical language need to be revised explicitly with the student. In addition, the student requires some assistance in the following areas. If similar patterns emerge through the diagnostic assessment of other responses to the task, the following strategies could be incorporated into teaching programs.

STRUCTURAL FEATURES OF EXPLANATIONS

The typical structure of an explanation includes a description stage followed by an explanatory sequence with an optional interpretation/evaluation, although this was not an essential requirement for this task. The structure can be assessed at three levels: the text introduces the explanation by classifying and describing the phenomenon, the text has an explanatory sequence that elaborates by explaining how and why, and the text includes some interpretation/evaluation.

In order to explicitly teach the structural features of an explanation, consider the following strategies:

- Model the explanation on *Flotation* used earlier in this chapter or something similar.

- Ask the class to identify the description stage. Point out that a description tells us what something is and what it is like. Draw on student's knowledge of the structural features of describing to do this.

- Now have them identify the classification.

- Ask why an explanation needs a description stage first.
  - It classifies the phenomenon as a part or member of a particular group of thing.

- It describes how the phenomenon fits into or is different from other things within the same network.
- It describes essential features or uses that are relevant to the subsequent explanatory sequence.

- Have the class examine their own explanations and identify whether they have a description stage.

- Next move onto the explanatory sequence. As a class activity, have the students identify the action verbs. Discuss how the explanatory sequence links together the processes or verbs. In identifying the action verbs, you will find that you are also identifying the key content words for the explanatory sequence.

DEVELOPING BASIC SENTENCE STRUCTURE

The following strategies will examine the construction of effective compound sentences. Strategies for the construction of complex sentences will be covered in the assessment strategies in Chapter 6.

- Discuss compound sentences with the class. Point out that compound sentences have two or more clauses that are joined in an equal relationship, such as:

   Pollution damages the environment *and* it is a waste of resources.

- Point out how each clause is providing a separate piece of information that is independent of the other. In other words, they could each be sentences in their own right.

- Ask what the word *and* is doing in the sentence – it is joining the pieces of information together by adding one clause to the other clause. It is therefore called an additive conjunction.

- For an individual writing activity, have students construct compound sentences using the following additive conjunctions:

   also   as well as
   in addition   furthermore
   besides

UNDERSTANDING THE SUBJECT–VERB–OBJECT (SVO) PATTERN

It is important to explicitly explain to students the SVO nature of English clause structures. The following activities focus on the requirement for every main clause or simple sentence to have a finite verb.

- First focus on what a simple sentence is – it is a group of words that makes complete sense. It also starts with a capital letter and ends with a full stop, exclamation mark or question mark.

- Discuss what a sentence does – it tells us about something 'going on' or. The part that tells what is happening or what it 'is' or 'has' is called a verb. Display a list of simple sentences dealing with actions and have the class identify the verbs. For example,

  At the factory workers *sort* the paper.
  They then *move* further down the line.

- Use examples of a sentence and non-sentence like the following and ask the class whether they are sentences or not. Discuss why one is not a sentence – it doesn't make complete sense.

  | Recycling paper is very important. | Sentence |
  | The procedure in your house | Non-sentence |

- Ask what the non-sentence would need to make complete sense. In other words, what is missing? – Something that says what is happening, a word like 'starts' or 'begins'. For example,

  The procedure *starts* in your house.

  Both of these words are not only verbs but finite verbs.
  See Chapter 2 for information on finite verbs.

- Point out how every sentence must have a finite verb. Conduct exercises with students where they identify finite verbs in sentences.

- Make a list of sentences and non-sentences and as an individual or group activity, have students identify the sentences and what is missing from the non-sentences.

- Now have students return to their own explanations and check them to see if each main clause has a finite verb.

After completing these exercises have students redraft their explanation. Alternatively, provide students with another assessment task on writing a technical explanation.

CHAPTER 6

THE GENRE
OF INSTRUCTING

The genre of instructing, whether spoken or written, pervades our experience of the world. To bake a cake, program a VCR, or find our way to a new and unfamiliar destination, we need to be competent in this genre. However, instructing involves much more than simple, sequential or procedural texts. While the purpose of instructing is to tell someone what to do or how to do it, this can be achieved through a range of textual forms.

A recipe for a carrot cake and a pamphlet encouraging householders to be environmentally aware are clearly both about doing something, yet the form and function of each text is quite different. The recipe is sequential and makes use of imperatives:

Firstly cream the butter, then add the beaten egg.

The pamphlet may not be sequential. Furthermore, it is unlikely, since it presents an environmental alternative to householders, that it would be written as a set of commands:

> Oil and water don't mix. It is not a good idea to pour oil down the drain. Why not collect kitchen oils and store in a container?

Clearly, we don't always get people to follow instructions by issuing orders. Consequently, some instructional texts make use of the language of persuasion. In such cases, instructing resembles the genre of arguing, a language process discussed in the next chapter.

Children are similarly confronted with a range of instructional texts both at home and at school. From their earliest years, they become familiar with spoken instructions such as, 'Eat up all your dinner', 'Make sure you pull the chain', and on into school with 'Come in and sit down quietly', 'Put up your hand when you want to answer a question'. Familiarity with the spoken forms of the genre provides a sound basis for the development of written instructional texts across the curriculum throughout the K-6 years, such as the following types of writing:

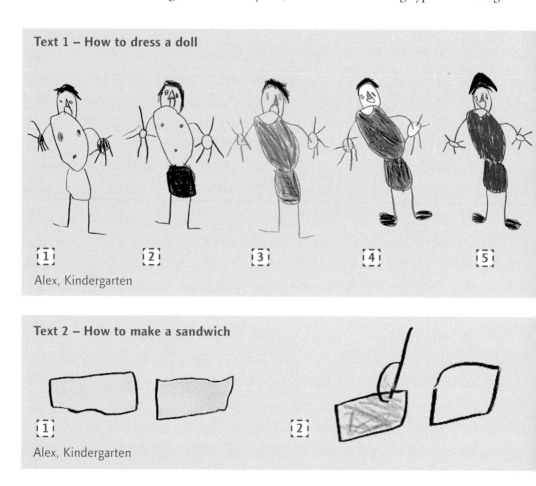

Text 1 – How to dress a doll

`1`   `2`   `3`   `4`   `5`

Alex, Kindergarten

Text 2 – How to make a sandwich

`1`   `2`

Alex, Kindergarten

- an experiment on osmosis in Science

- instructions to make an origami figure in Creative Arts

- a guide to planting a tree for Environmental Education

- directions on how to operate the class computer for Technology

- a recipe for a witches' brew in English

- the procedure to follow for long division in Maths

- a pamphlet on hints for good nutrition in Health.

EARLY PROCEDURAL TEXTS/CONCRETE EXPERIENCES

One of the early cognitive skills children develop is the ability to sequence. However, many children flounder when they are expected to reproduce a sequence of steps in writing. For this reason it is important to use concrete activities when first working with instructing and to represent stages in a procedure pictorially. Children then begin to make direct links between a concrete action and its graphic representation, initially through pictures and eventually with the written text.

It is at this point that children can be introduced to the structure and grammar of procedural instructions. Opposite and below are two examples of early procedural texts that were completed by kindergarten children after participating in the concrete tasks of dressing a doll and making a sandwich.

These two texts highlight the key structural feature of procedural texts – the sequence of steps. Text 1 shows the steps involved in dressing a doll. Step 1 shows the undressed doll, followed by the doll wearing pants, then a T-shirt, next a hat, and finally shoes. Text 2 illustrates the process of making a sandwich: take two pieces of bread, spread them with butter and jam, put them together and

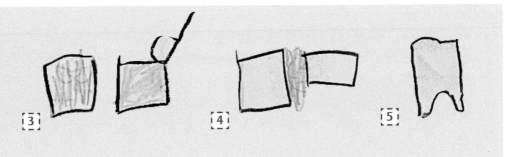

finally take a bite. The texts also indicate an ability to deal with aspects of the grammar of instructing, such as the processes involved in each step, represented by action verbs, and the temporal nature of the sequencing, represented in the grammar by temporal connectives.

GRAMMATICAL FEATURES OF INSTRUCTIONS

- The notion of address is a key feature of instructing. The addressee may be referred to either directly or indirectly; for example,

	Direct Address
Judith, put the rubbish in the bin.	Addressee specified by name (more characteristic of spoken instructions)
You, put the rubbish in the bin.	Use of second person pronoun

	Indirect Address
( ) Put the rubbish in the bin.	Addressee ellipted
It is important to put the rubbish in the bin.	Use of third person pronoun (It) Passive voice

- Action verbs are used in instructions to represent the processes involved in completing a task; for example,

  Cross Smith Street and turn right.
  Walk to the next cross street.

- Verbs are in the simple present tense to create a sense of timelessness. They are also stated as imperatives.

- Adverbs are often used to qualify verbs and to provide extra information about how a task should be completed; for example,

  Slowly, add the remaining ingredients.
  Walk *quickly* across the road.

- Temporal connectives are used in procedural instructions to ensure processes are placed in the correct order of time; for example,

  First melt the butter, *then* add the flour.

- Conditional connectives are used to provide a premise upon which a command or statement is based; for example,

  If you get stuck in a traffic jam that is not moving, turn the engine off.
  If you mix the ingredients carefully, there won't be any lumps.

- Modality is used in instructions to lessen or heighten the degree of obligation in completing a task; for example,

  You *should* save your document before closing.
  You *might like* to close the door before you leave.
  You *could* read the next section of the book after completing your work.

THE STRUCTURE OF INSTRUCTIONS

PROCEDURAL INSTRUCTIONS

Procedural instructions such as recipes and directions are concerned with telling someone how to do something. For this reason, procedural texts generally begin with the goal of the task, which is usually stated as a heading; for example, 'How to Make a Sandwich' or 'Directions for Using the Class Computer'. Following this stage, a set of ingredients or the materials required to complete the task will often be presented in the order of use. Some instructions, such as directions to use an appliance, may not include this information. The text then proceeds through a sequence of steps specifying how the goal is to be achieved. The steps may be accompanied by illustrations or diagrams to assist the reader with the task at hand. Some texts may include comments at certain stages of the procedure. These three stages – goal, materials and sequence of steps – are shown in the procedures on page 158.

Chocolate Crackles	Goal
Ingredients Four cup of ris bubles one cup of iceing shoger 200 and 50 grams copho three tabble spoon of cocoe one cup of cocoenut	Materials/ ingredients
How to make melt the copho then por the copho with the uder stuf then ster it up then spoon into the paty pan then put it in the fridge till redy Year 1	Sequence of steps
How to Play Snakes and Ladders	Goal
What you need Snakes and Ladders board game 1 dice 2, 3, 4 players Counters of different colours. 1 for each player.	Materials
How to Play • Put all counters on start. • First person rolls the dice and moves his counter in counting order the number of places shown on the dice. • Other players take their turns. • If a counter lands on the bottom of a ladder, the player moves the counter to the top of that ladder. • If a counter lands on a snake's head, the player moves the counter down to the bottom of that snake's tail. • The winner is the first player to reach Finish. Year 5	Sequence of steps

NON-PROCEDURAL INSTRUCTIONS

While the structural features of procedural instructions are easily specifiable, instructions that are not sequential take a range of textual forms, and hence, vary structurally. What tends to characterise non-procedural instructions is not their structural features but their grammar. However, there are certain similarities in how they are structured rhetorically in order to position the reader, which are evident in the texts below.

Ten Ways to Save Petrol

1. Drive smoothly, do not race the other cars to the next red light.
2. Are all the accessories necessary, eg, roof rack, bull bar, tow bar, etc? They can cause extra weight and drag.
3. Always choose the best route and time, eg, don't drive in the rush hour (if possible) and avoid big intersections.
4. Airconditioning uses up an extra 10% of petrol.
5. Use public transport when you can. Is it necessary to take your car, somebody else might be going to the same place and you could get a lift.
6. Don't get into the habit of resting your foot on the brake or clutch. Another bad habit is to rev the engine before you turn the ignition off.
7. Always use the correct gear, eg, going up a steep hill don't use a high gear and don't use a low gear when on the open road.
8. Don't leave the choke out too long.
9. If you get stuck in a traffic jam that is not moving turn the engine off.
10. Make sure the car is in good working order.

Year 6

Jury Deliberation

Like any group of people who meet for the purpose of determining a matter, solving a problem or reading a decision, the members of a jury must approach their task in a positive and organised manner.

It is essential in such a meeting that each member interacts with, and respects the opinions of the others. Each member should listen to others and be permitted to have their say.

It is important that one or two persons do not dominate the discussion and when necessary others must be encouraged to participate. At appropriate times it may be advantageous for suggestions and views to be summarised.

Remember that the jury deliberating process is a decision making process and its success rests largely with the participants. Each juror must be permitted to enter into discussion enthusiastically, and each person's view must be respected.

Extract from Jury Duty – *A rewarding responsibility*,
Office of the Sheriff of NSW.

These two texts are generically instructions, yet at first glance their only common structural feature is the goal; that is, 'Ten Ways to Save Petrol' and 'Jury Deliberation'. A closer reading, however, reveals an interesting interplay between the use of imperatives, questions and propositions, which is more pronounced in 'Ten Ways to Save Petrol' but is common to both texts. For example:

Drive smoothly, do not race the other cars to the next red light.	Imperative
Are all the accessories necessary, eg, roof rack, bull bar, towbar, etc?	Question
Airconditioning uses up an extra 10% of petrol.	Proposition
It is essential in such a meeting that each member interacts …	Proposition
Remember that the jury deliberating process is a decision making process …	Imperative

The structure of these texts has therefore quite an overt rhetorical function; that is, to provide options to the reader rather than to instruct in a dogmatic fashion through a reliance on imperatives. The extent to which this feature is used is clearly related to the purpose and audience, but is evident in a wide variety of non-procedural instructions.

THE GRAMMAR OF INSTRUCTING

PICTURE GRAMMAR

We use language to represent our experience of the world. Grammar is a resource for organising this experience in language. The real-life experiences of performing certain concrete tasks, such as preparing food, can be represented in language through the grammar of instructing. Children first meet aspects of this grammar at school through illustrations of sequential activities. For instance, each step in the visual representation of making a sandwich signifies a process or action verb (*italicised*):

The order of these steps can also be indicated in the grammar through temporal connectives (italicised) as follows:

THE GRAMMAR OF PROCEDURES

The text below, by a Year 2 student, represents the process of making a sandwich using written language. The list of ingredients is composed of common nouns – *bread, butter, lettuce* – which are then incorporated in the process of making the sandwich. Each step in the process is represented by an action verb – *take, spread, put* – expressed in the simple present tense. These actions are stated as imperatives, with the addressee referred to both directly and indirectly at different stages of the text; for example, *You take* (direct) *and spread butter* (indirect).

Students often have difficulty with the notion of address and the use of present tense in their first attempts at writing instructions, as they are generally more familiar with recounting personal experiences which make use of the first person pronoun *I* and past tense; for example, *went*. Comparing the different textual forms of recount and instruction, and drawing attention to their different purposes – that is, of telling someone what you have done (a *recount*) and telling someone else how to do something (an *instruction*) – clarifies the grammatical differences.

It is interesting in the following text that the writer has chosen to indicate the order of steps by using numerals rather than temporal connectives, with the exception of *Next* in step 3.

How to make a Salid Sandwitch

Ingredients
2 pieces of bread
butter
lettace
tomato
beetroot
cucumba
and others

1. You take 2 pieces of bread.
2. Spread butter on the bread.
3. Next put in your lettace, tomato, beetroot and cucumba or any other ingredients.
4. Put the other piece of bread on top.
5. Put on plate and give it to your mum!

Year 2

The following set of instructions similarly makes use of imperatives – *walk, turn, regulate, get* – yet unlike the previous text, there is some use of modality, providing options in the process of having a shower: *You might like to use shampoo if your hair is dirty, You can use powder if you want*. Modality is also used to heighten the degree of obligation, rather than simply relying on the imperative to perform this function: *You should wash it out really well*.

There is use of both direct and indirect address throughout the text, with theme position given to a range of grammatical classes, such as the second person pronoun *you*, imperatives such as *walk, turn, rub*, and also the temporal connective *then*. It is typical of many students' texts that there is an overuse of *then*.

The writer has used a range of action verbs in the present tense to represent the steps in taking a shower. In some cases they have been qualified by adverbs: *turn on the shower **slowly**, wash out the shampoo **carefully***.

How to Have a Shower
Walk into the bathroom and get undressed. Turn on the shower slowly so you don't burn yourself and regulate it until you have it the temperature you want it to be. Then get into the shower and wash yourself. Get a piece of soap and a sponge and wash yourself where you think you need it most.

If your hair is dirty get some shampoo and put a little bit on your hand and rub it into your hair. Then wash out the shampoo carefully so it doesn't get into your eyes. You might need to use conditioner. If you do put a bit on your hand and rub it into your hair. You should wash it out really well so your hair isn't greasy. Rinse your whole body from the soap.

When you have finished turn off the shower pick up the towel and dry yourself. You can use powder if you what. Then put on your clothes and now you are clean and fresh.

Year 4

THE GRAMMAR OF NON-PROCEDURAL INSTRUCTIONS

Although a set of instructions, the text below is not a procedure. The numerals used in the text do not signify time, and there are no temporal connectives. It is an instructional text, as it is telling the reader how to do something, yet there is limited use of direct address. In most cases the address is understood. There is, however, consistent use of imperatives, a common feature of instructing.

There is also evidence of some of the rhetorical devices used in argument. These include questioning – *Are all the accessories necessary?* – and propositions – *They can cause extra weight and drag*; and *Air conditioning uses up an extra 10% of petrol.* These devices are used to provide the reader with options in following the instructions, so that the writer appears reasonable rather than bullying. This use of the language of persuasion to achieve a greater degree of optionality in the text is generally more characteristic of non-procedural instructions. In many procedures, such as 'How to Play Snakes and Ladders', there are no options.

Ten Ways to Save Petrol

1. Drive smoothly, do not race the other cars to the next red light.
2. Are all the accessories necessary, eg, roof rack, bull bar, tow bar, etc. They can cause extra weight and drag.
3. Always choose the best route and time, eg, don't drive in the rush hour (if possible) and avoid big intersections.
4. Airconditioning uses up an extra 10% of petrol.
5. Use public transport when you can. Is it necessary to take your car, somebody else might be going to the same place and you could get a lift.
6. Don't get into the habit of resting your foot on the brake or clutch. Another bad habit is to rev the engine before you turn the ignition off.
7. Always use the correct gear, eg, going up a steep hill don't use a high gear and don't use a low gear when on the open road.
8. Don't leave the choke out too long.
9. If you get stuck in a traffic jam that is not moving turn the engine off.
10. Make sure the car is in good working order.

Year 6

The 'Jury Deliberation' text is included to demonstrate further the links between instructing and arguing, and to highlight the fluid nature of the language processes with which we are working.

Jury Deliberation

Like any group of people who meet for the purpose of determining a matter, solving a problem or reading a decision, the members of a jury must approach their task in a positive and organised manner.

It is essential in such a meeting that each member interacts with, and respects the opinions of the others. Each member should listen to others and be permitted to have their say.

It is important that one or two persons do not dominate the discussion and when necessary others must be encouraged to participate. At appropriate times it may be advantageous for suggestions and views to be summarised.

Remember that the jury deliberating process is a decision making process and its success rests largely with the participants. Each juror must be permitted to enter into discussion enthusiastically, and each person's view must be respected.

Extract from *Jury Duty – A rewarding responsibility*,
Office of the Sheriff of NSW.

As with the previous text, this is a non-procedural instruction. In dealing with a sensitive topic such as jury deliberation, the writer of this text has been careful not to issue imperatives, with the exception of *Remember* in the first sentence of the last paragraph. However, as the aim of the text is to ensure that jurors work in an effective and collaborative way, modalities which indicate a high degree of obligation are used: *must, essential, should, important, dominate, necessary, largely*. Modalities, in fact, saturate the text and are found in a full range of grammatical categories:

should, must, may	Verbs (modal auxiliaries)
dominate, approach	Verbs
largely, enthusiastically	Adverbs
essential, important, necessary	Adjectives
suggestions	Nouns

The genre of instructing is used in a variety of ways in a range of text types. In the school context, it is not only evident in the texts students write, but also in many they read. Most textbooks make use of instructions. Having an understanding of the structural and grammatical features of instructing – indeed, all the genres of school writing – assists students with reading, as it equips them with the necessary semantic and syntactic clues to access meaning in texts.

TEACHING THE GENRE AND GRAMMAR OF INSTRUCTING

TARGET GROUP: YEARS 4/5

The following teaching ideas are based on an integrated unit of work entitled 'You Are What You Eat', which draws on the learning areas of PD/H/PE, Science and English. The central theme of the unit is nutrition. It begins with students developing an understanding of the topic through the following activities commencing with the more concrete engagement with knowledge before progression to abstract understandings:

- class brainstorming exercise on the functions of food

- compiling a record of food intake from the previous day or, alternatively, recording information in a seven-day food diary

- class and group reading and research activities on aspects of food and diet: the five food groups, food nutrients, a balanced diet, dietary disorders

- compiling a word bank of key 'nutrition' words

- listening to a guest speaker on nutrition

- examining nutritional information on food packaging

- completing flow charts on the digestive system

- role-plays on consultations with a dietitian to diagnose dietary disorders

- class callisthenics

- developing an individual exercise program.

Many of these activities involve describing and explaining, because it is these genres which largely deal with the 'what' and 'how' of a topic. It is important in developing a unit of work to give careful consideration to the relationship between language and knowledge in order to assist students in understanding content. Although motivated by good intentions, we may plan language-based activities that draw upon genres that are inappropriate for the content which is being treated. For instance, reading a story about a trip through the digestive system could be a useful stimulus, but expecting students to respond by writing their own story could be placing unrealistic language demands upon them, particularly in the early years of schooling. It could also create confusion in dealing with factual content, as school science does not lend itself to narrative. To complete such an activity successfully, students would be required to mesh the technical terminology and grammar of a scientific report with the quite different language demands of writing narrative. While this is possible – in fact, it is the essence of science fiction – we need to consider if it is appropriate when examining content from a factual perspective in the school context.

ANALYSING RECIPES

After developing an understanding of the topic of nutrition by completing the activities listed above, students can begin to consider other aspects of the topic, such as preparing food for a healthy diet.

- Ask students to bring recipes to class collected from magazines and have them paste these in their books. In groups, students can examine these recipes and assign ingredients to the five food groups.

- Have students rate the nutritional value of these recipes.

- Begin to examine the structure and grammar of these recipes with students in preparation for them writing their own texts. Students should re-read the recipes they have brought to class. Focus on the structure of these texts in a class discussion by asking the following questions:

  - Does each recipe have a heading?
  - Why is this important information for the reader?
  - What follows the heading (that is, the list of ingredients)?
  - Is there a particular order to the list of ingredients?
  - What is the next stage of the recipe (that is, the method)?
  - How is this information organised?
  - Is this section accompanied by illustrations?

- Record this information on a wall display for later reference.

- Take a closer look at the recipes by examining the grammar. Using an OHP, display a sample text, as below, and focus students' attention on the method stage of the recipe.

Muesli

Ingredients
750 grams of rolled oats
1 cup of barley flakes
1/2 cup of sesame seeds
1 cup of wheatgerm
2 cups of processed oat-bran cereal
1/2 cup of roasted buck wheat
250 grams of dried fruit medley
250 grams of sultanas
100 grams of banana chips
1/2 cup of sunflower seeds
milk and yogurt as required

1. Place half the oats on an ungreased oven tray.
2. Bake at 200°C for about 10–15 mins, carefully stirring several times, until golden brown.
3. Repeat with the remaining oats and barley.
4. Cool the grains.
5. Lightly toast the sesame seeds in a dry frying pan until golden brown and cool.
6. Combine all the ingredients and store in an airtight container.
7. Later serve with milk and yogurt for a hearty breakfast.

IDENTIFYING THE VERBS AND CONNECTIVES

Have students identify the action verbs in the text and record their responses on the board: *Place, Bake, Repeat, Cool.* An alternative strategy for students who are unfamiliar with this grammatical category is for the teacher to underline the action verbs in the text and ask students what these words are doing. Compare the action verbs with the nouns (things) in the text: *oats, oven tray, barley.* Discuss the relationship between the verb and the noun in a sentence, and the way the action verb indicates what is to be done with the noun: <u>bake</u> the oats, <u>cool</u> the grains.

Ask students to indicate any words that add extra information to the way the action verbs should be performed. This involves identifying adverbs such as *carefully* and *lightly*.

Have students consider the order in which the verbs are sequenced. Examine how the sequence of steps is indicated in the text through the use of numerals. Using the OHP, display the text shown below, which is a recipe that uses temporal connectives rather than numerals to indicate the order of steps.

Apricot Slice

Ingredients
1 cup of chopped dried apricots
1/2 cup of sultanas
1/2 cup of chopped prunes, pitted
1/2 cup of orange juice
1 cup of mik powder
1/2 cup fresh wholemeal breadcrumbs
1/2 cup chopped almonds
1/4 cup desiccated coconut

First, combine the apricots, sultanas, prunes, and orange juice. Then bring the mixture to the boil, cover and leave to stand for 15 minutes. Next add the milk powder, bread crumbs and almonds, and mix thoroughly. Sprinkle half the coconut over the base of a non-stick shallow pan about 25 cm × 18 cm. Then press the mixture into the pan and sprinkle with the remaining coconut, pressing it in well. Finally cover and leave in the fridge for several hours before cutting into small slices to serve.

Ask students to identify the temporal connectives or 'time words' – *First, Then, Next* – and record their responses on the board.

Distribute a grid, such as the following, to students and ask them to read through the recipes they have brought to class and identify the action verbs, adverbs and temporal connectives in these texts.

Action verbs	Adverbs	Temporal connectives

This exercise can also function as a self-assessment task to determine whether students understand these grammatical terms.

To reinforce these concepts, make a healthy treat in class. This provides a concrete activity which students can use as a basis for constructing a written text. This can be conducted as a class exercise with the teacher as cook and the students taking notes on the sequence of steps involved in completing the task.

Following this practical activity, have students write up the recipe they have just seen prepared, using the scaffold below as a guide. Remind students about correctly sequencing their action verbs.

Heading or Goal	
Ingredients (in order of use)	
Method	

COMPARING AND CONTRASTING STUDENT TEXTS

Select two or three of these texts for discussion with the class. Consider how each text has been structured. Take a closer look at the method stage. Discuss how the action verbs and temporal connectives have been used. Have the writers used adverbs?

Also ask students how each of the sentences in the method stage of each text begins. See if a pattern has emerged with the first or theme position of the sentences. Generally, recipes begin with an action verb used as an imperative or with a temporal connective. Discuss with students the reasons why this might be the case. Some students may have thematised the second person pronoun *you*. Have students examine their own recipes to see if they have used the word *you*.

To focus on the notion of address in instructing, ask the following questions:

- Who is the 'you' referred to in the text? (the reader)
- Why would a recipe often make direct reference to the reader by using the word 'you'?
- What has happened to the word 'you' in the Muesli recipe? (it is ellipsed or understood)
- Does a writer need to use the word 'you' in a recipe to address the reader?
- How is the reader addressed in the Muesli recipe? (through the use of imperatives – 'you' is understood)

• Display the following four sentences using an OHP and ask students to explain in what way they are different.

1   Blend the sugar and the butter.
2   The sugar is blended with the butter.
3   Should the sugar be blended with the butter?
4   Look, the sugar is being blended with the butter!

• Assign names to these different types of sentences and indicate how they use different punctuation signs:

1   Command   (.)
2   Statement   (.)
3   Question   (?)
4   Exclamation   (!)

• Ask students why commands are the most common sentences used in recipes. Also discuss what other types of sentences would be used in a recipe – usually statements.

ANALYSING AND REDRAFTING

Following this examination of address, theme and sentence type, ask students to consider these features and to redraft their recipes. It is at this point that non-procedural instructions can be introduced to the class.

Refocus students' attention on the topic of the unit – nutrition. Apart from recipe books, ask students where else people might find information about food and nutrition – library books, TV shows, pamphlets from the doctor or dentist.

- Introduce the class assignment, which is to write a guide on good nutrition which could be displayed at the local doctor's surgery.

- Drawing on their knowledge of the topic, have students in groups discuss what they consider to be useful information to include in a guide to good nutrition. Ask each group to compile a list of ten points on butcher's paper.

- Discuss each group's response and display these points on the wall chart for later reference. Explain to students that while they have information for their guide, they must consider how the guide will be written. Begin to discuss the format with students by asking the following focus question:

> A guide and a recipe have a similar purpose – they are both designed to tell someone how to do something. Does this mean that the format and language used in recipes and guides are the same?

To assist students in answering this question, display the text shown below and discuss.

> **How to Take Care of a Puppy**
> 1. Give him a bath every fortnight.
> 2. It is a good idea to brush him and use some flea powder.
> 3. Make sure he wears a collar.
> 4. He might need a smack if he barks too much.
> 5. Make sure he has fresh water every day.
> 6. Give him a warm rug to use when it is cold.
> 7. Check he doesn't have ticks.
> 8. Take him for a walk every day.
> 9. Dogs need a balanced diet just like people.
> 10. Why not give him a special treat now and then.
> Year 4

- Pose the following questions to aid discussion:
  - How do the formats of the guide and the recipe differ?
  - What do the numerals in the puppy text represent? Are they used in the same way as in the Muesli recipe – that is, do they represent a sequence of steps in terms of time?
  - Would temporal connectives be used in a guide?
  - Are all the sentences commands?
  - Are other types of sentences used?

- – Why might a guide use statements more often than a recipe? (purpose is to inform as well as instruct)
  – What is the effect of using a question? (gives the reader the option of agreeing or disagreeing)
- Following this discussion, have students write the first draft of a guide to good nutrition, using the scaffold below:

Heading	
Points	
1	
2	
3	
4	
5	
6	
7	
8	
9	
10	

Remind students that while a guide aims to instruct, it is also a text designed to inform. While imperatives can be used, a non-procedural text is not as reliant on commands as is a recipe. The reader may not respond to orders. A guide might therefore make use of language that persuades rather than orders. This will have an effect on the sentence type and also on the use of modality.

After students have completed a draft, compare and contrast selected texts. A sample response is shown on the next page:

A Guide to Good Nutrition

1. Eat lots of fruit and vegetables. It is important to have either a piece of fruit or vegetables with each meal of the day.
2. Instead of sweet treats like lollies or cakes, why not eat an apple or banana?
3. Cereals or bread should also be eaten with each meal of the day.
4. Milk products and meat are important sources of protein but they can also be fatty. Be sure not to eat too many milk products and trim fat from meat.
5. Eat lots of fish.
6. Don't eat too much salt, sugar or fatty foods.
7. Check additives in processed foods and if possible choose unprocessed food products.
8. Don't eat too much take-away food.
9. Drink plenty of water and fruit juice.
10. Exercise daily.

Year 4

Following a discussion of the structure and grammar of the first draft of their guide, have students redraft their work for a final copy.

ASSESSING TEXTS USING THE GENRE OF INSTRUCTING – A NON-PROCEDURAL INSTRUCTION

OUTLINE OF THE TASK

The following diagnostic assessment task required Year 8 students to write a set of instructions for students intending to go on an overnight bush camp. Students were told that they were required to write more than a list of instructions. The task shown below outlines how the writing requires elaborations to the instructions so that readers will understand the reasons for taking the necessary equipment and following the required procedures. The stimulus for the task includes a list of essential items to take and the text is modelled by having the first heading and instruction already written. The modelled instruction includes an elaboration telling readers why it is necessary to notify the school, park rangers and family of the intended camp location. Students were also given visual stimulus by way of pictures of the types of equipment that should be taken for the camp.

> Write a set of instructions to help your class prepare for an overnight camp in a national park. The instructions should tell people what to do and not to do and also give reasons for the instructions. For example,
>
> When preparing for your camp you should first contact the National Parks and Wildlife Service to get permission. The rangers will be able to provide you with useful information on current conditions in the park and advise you on suitable camping locations.
>
> The following is a list of essential items that campers should take on the camp.
>
> A map
> A compass
> A sleeping bag
> A tent
> A raincoat
> Warm clothing
> Plenty of water
> Ample food
> Plastic bags for rubbish
> A torch.
>
> NSW Parks & Wildlife Service, General Safety Information

Students were told to organise their writing using headings, to write in sentences that are well structured and make sense, to pay attention to spelling and punctuation, and to use the editing time to review their writing.

While the focus of this task is to diagnostically assess students' ability to harness the structural and grammatical resources of the genre of instructing, the task also assessed students' performance on aspects of writing common to all written texts; namely, syntax, punctuation and spelling.

The task specifically asked students to write a non-sequenced or non-procedural set of instructions. Earlier in this chapter the features of non-procedural instructions were outlined including some of their salient structural and grammatical features. Non-procedural instructions, for example, often include declarative sentences that elaborate or rationalise why particular things need to be done. The *Ten Ways to Save Petrol* and *Jury Deliberation* texts demonstrate the use of rhetorical devices such as modality, rhetorical questions and nominalisations.

The *School Camp* writing task requires a similar degree of modality to ensure readers accept the obligation to carefully follow the instructions. The modelled writing uses a high degree of modality in the direct instruction – <u>*Don't*</u> *leave the camp area without notifying someone* ... – and a lower degree of modality when rationalising why this should be done – <u>*If*</u> *something happens* ... The model also indicates to students that the text requires appropriate structure in terms of headings and formatting.

The following are the assessment criteria used for assessing the task based on the appropriate generic structural and grammatical features described earlier in the chapter.

1 *Genre-based* criteria deal with the macro level features of the text. This level covers these criteria:
   – does the writing instruct/advise?
   – is the theme of the writing consistent with the task?
   – does the text use appropriate modality?
   – is the structure or staging of the text consistent with the genre?

2 *Textual language* criteria deal with the way that the text is held together, the way that sentences are structured and how sentences work with one another. This level covers the next three criteria:
   – is the text formatted appropriately?
   – does the text use correctly structured simple, compound and complex sentences?
   – does the text use tense appropriately and consistently?

3 *Syntactical language* criteria deal with the internal structure of the sentences used. This level covers the next five criteria:
   – do all main clauses have essential elements such as a main verb and do statements have the subject and main verb in the correct order?
   – do the subject and main verb agree in person and number?
   – are prepositions used appropriately and with some variety?
   – are articles and plurals used correctly?
   – is sentence, simple and complex punctuation correct?

4 *Spelling* deals with the way that individual words are spelt.
   – are most high-frequency words spelt correctly?
   – are most less frequently used words and words with common but not simple patterns spelt correctly?

- are most words with difficult or unusual patterns spelt correctly?
- are most challenging words appropriate to the task spelt correctly?
- are all challenging words appropriate to the task spelt correctly?

What you need

1 First you will need food. You should take a lot
of this so if you get hungry you have all
food needed.
Also a map will be needed, so you don't get
5 lost.
A torch will be needed, for night time so you
can see where you are going.
A compass will also be used to know
where you are, and you know were north,
10 south, east and west is.
A pocket knife will be needed if your
in a bit of trouble doing something.
Finally sleeping bag will be needed to keep
your self warm on cold nights.
15 SHOULD
You should take all these things to live
on your school camp.
SHOULDN'T
You shouldn't take too much because of
20 the weight on you, it will bee too much for
you to carry. You will get too tired
very quickly.
So only takes things you need.

GENRE

GENRE AND THEME

The writing mainly instructs and advises.
The theme is consistent with the task.

TEXT STRUCTURE AND FORMATTING

The instructions include some elaborations. The text is organised with only basic headings and instructions beginning on a new line, although the headings are inadequate for the task (l. 15, l. 18).

MODALITY

There is only limited use of modal auxiliaries of obligation (l. 1 *should*, l. 16 *should*, l. 19 *shouldn't*), probability (l. 7 *can*) and modal adverbs (l. 2 *if*, l. 11 *if*).

TEXTUAL LANGUAGE

SENTENCE STRUCTURE

The writing attempts to use complex sentences with more than one dependent relationship and while most are successful from a structural point of view, not all succeed semantically (l. 8 *A compass will also be used* …, l. 16, *You should take all these things* …)

TENSE

Tense is generally consistent although there is inappropriate use of tense in a conditional clause (l. 2 *you [will] have*).

SYNTACTICAL LANGUAGE

CLAUSE PATTERN

Sentences always have a main clause and all finite clauses have a subject and finite verb.

AGREEMENT

Most verb forms agree with their subjects (l. 23 *So only take[s]*).

ARTICLES

Articles have been omitted where needed (l. 3 *you have all [the] food needed*, l. 13 *Finally [a] sleeping bag*, l. 23 *So only takes [the] things*).

PREPOSITIONS

The writing makes limited use of prepositions and does not indicate the use of a necessary preposition following a phrasal verb (l. 16 *all these things to live on [during/on] your school camp*) and uses an prepositional phrase (l. 20 *the weight [on you]*).

PUNCTUATION

Most sentence and simple punctuation is correct, although there is evidence of the omission of an apostrophe (l.11 *your [you're]*).

SPELLING

Most words with two and three syllables with common patterns are spelt correctly, although there is some confusion with homophones (l.11 *your, you're*, l. 20 *bee, be*).

SUMMARY

This text demonstrates a basic understanding of the genre by following the task and model, and attempting the appropriate formatting and organisation. The writing instructs and advises, although there is only a limited use of modalities. The writing demonstrates a suitable level of sentence structure and syntax, although not all complex sentences are successful. Most words are spelt correctly, although some simple words are incorrect. Most sentence and simple punctuation is correct, although there are some basic errors in sentence punctuation and little control of the use of commas and apostrophes.

TEACHING STRATEGIES BASED ON DIAGNOSTIC ASSESSMENT

Teaching strategies similar to those described earlier in the chapter on genre, structure and rhetorical strategies need to be revised explicitly with the student. In addition, the student requires some assistance in the following areas. If similar patterns emerge through the diagnostic assessment of other students' responses to the task, the following strategies could be incorporated into teaching programs.

ORGANISING INSTRUCTIONS LOGICALLY WITH ELABORATIONS

While the writer was able to write instructions that provided limited reasons for campers to follow what was being said, the writing was far less successful at organising the instructions in a logical order.

• As was pointed out earlier in this chapter, procedural and non-procedural instructions follow an entirely different logic – procedural instructions follow a temporal sequence, whereas as non-procedural instructions follow a rational logic. To examine this point, display some examples of procedural instructions such as recipes or computer hardware/software instructions and discuss the following:

- Procedural instructions are organised in temporal sequences that are identified by: the use of numbers such as 1, 2, 3 and so on; or, temporal conjunctions such as *then, when, next, before* and so on.
- The instructions mainly tell the reader what to do to achieve their goal.

• Now display a non-procedural instruction such as the following and discuss any differences with the class. For example,

General safety information
Whenever you visit a park or reserve, please follow these guidelines:

Planning your visit
Contact the park office to ask about local conditions, tracks, creek or river water levels and fire danger. During hot, dry periods a Total Fire Ban may be declared in the park. At such times you will not be able to cook anything – no fire or fuel stoves can be lit. You'll need to bring pre-cooked or fresh food.

Make sure you will have at least three people in your group. If there is an emergency, at least one can go for help, while the other stays with the injured or ill person.

Make sure there's at least one experienced person in the group who can guide and assist others.

Make sure your activity is something which all participants in your group are able to do.

Before heading out, leave full details with a relative or a responsible person of where you will be going, who is with you, what equipment you have, and when you expect to return.

Allow plenty of time to finish the activity in daylight, and pack extra food and water in case of unexpected delays.

At the very least, make sure you have:
– matches
– topographic map(s)
– a compass
– a space blanket
– a first aid kit
– raincoats for everyone in the group
– warm clothing for everyone in the group
– plastic bags for rubbish

- plenty of water
- ample food
- torches.

Weather can change rapidly. Be prepared for heat, rain, thick mist, icy winds, and sleet or snow in mountain areas.

Many parks have only limited mobile phone coverage. If you intend to use a mobile for safety purposes, contact your phone network supplier to check the coverage in the park you intend to visit.

- Ask the class whether the headings organise the text into logical groupings of information for visitors and campers in national parks.

- Discuss the headings used in the sample text.
  - Ask whether the headings clearly signify the information organised under them.
  - Ask the class whether they can think of alternative headings that would do the same job.
  - Ask the class to think of any other instructions and elaborations that would be suitable for each of the headings.

- Point out how instructions often begin with a verb because they are commands and the subject is understood or ellipted. If students are unaware of the four different sentence types it may be useful to provide them with the following information.

Sentence Type	Example
The bell is ringing.	Statement
Is the bell ringing?	Question
Ring the bell.	Command
Look, the bell is ringing!	Exclamation

- Point out the differences between the sentences. Firstly focus on their functions:

  - a statement makes a claim or states something
  - a question asks for something or seeks information
  - a command demands or orders something
  - an exclamation emphasises or stresses something.

- Now point out the different positions of the finite and subject in the sentence types.

Example	Sentence type	Finite	Subject	Rule
The bell is ringing	Statement	is	The bell	The subject appears before the finite
Is the bell ringing?	Question	is	the bell	The subject appears after the finite
Ring the bell	Command	Ring	(you)	The subject 'you' can be left out or ellipted because it is understood

- Jointly identify which sentences or clauses are simply instructions and which provide elaboration. For example,

  Remember to take a new reliable map when camping (instruction) *so you know where you are going. This will prevent you hopefully from getting lost* and *should warn you of any obstacles and the difficulty of the hike* (elaboration).

- Now have the class individually or in groups identify the commands and statements in the rest of the sample text.
- To reinforce the structural elements of non-procedural instructions, display the model texts provided in the introduction and ask students to identify the instructions and elaborations (commands and statements).

MODALITY

Effective instructions seek to rhetorically position readers to obligingly follow the instructions. For example,

  You *must* check that everything you need has been packed before you leave.
  You *should* also inform the National Parks office of your plans.
  Modal auxiliaries expressing obligation

compared with

  Make sure that all essential items are packed. It *may* be necessary to use a checklist.
  Leave your intended route with the National Parks office as it *could* be useful if any problems arise.
  Modal auxiliaries expressing probability

- Discuss these examples with the class. Pay attention to the different types of modality – obligation and probability. Point out that modalities of obligation are most often used in sentences that are commands, whereas sentences that elaborate on the commands (sentences that are statements) will tend to use modalities of probability.

- Next point out that modalities can express degrees of obligation or probability. For example, *must* expresses a higher or stronger sense of obligation than does *should*.

- As an individual or group exercise, provide students with some examples of non-procedural instructions and have them identify any modal auxiliaries and indicate whether they are expressing obligation or probability. Various guides found in municipal libraries are a useful source of these types of texts.

- Modality can also be expressed through the use of adverbs such as: *perhaps, sometimes, if, certainly, usually, only, possibly, probably, maybe, definitely, obviously, quite, almost, hardly, really, actually, just* and so on. Modal adverbs such as these are generally used at the beginning of a sentence or clause and are used to qualify the truth or certainty of the statement that follows. Rhetorically this has the effect of making the statement seem more reasoned or open to interpretation and therefore more likely to be accepted by the reader.

- As a class activity, jointly construct sentences using each of the modal adverbs above. Then rewrite each sentence without the adverb and compare them noting the rhetorical effect the modal adverb.

- Modality can also be expressed through the use of other grammatical elements. For example, a modality can be expressed as an introductory clause to a statement with the degree of modality expressed through the use of an adjective. For example,

  > *It is possible* that the weather could change.
  > *One thing is certain*, you will need to take enough water.

- Expressing a modality in this way through the use of adjectives helps to provide an effective distance between the writer and reader of a non-procedural instruction. The rhetorical effect of such a strategy is to have the readers feel that they are not being told or ordered to do a particular thing. Instead they are invited to use their own reason to make the appropriate decision. There are a range of adjectives that can be used to express a modality. For example,

probable   possible
certain   usual
rare   willing
ready   easy
definite   absolute
sure   obvious
clear   simple
entire   utter

- As a class or individual activity have students use the above adjectives to express a degree of modality in sentences.

SENTENCE STRUCTURE

Often commands are simple sentences and only use a main clause. For example,

Always camp in a safe place.

Compound sentences have two main or independent clauses of equal status. The independent clauses are joined together with coordinating conjunctions such as *and, but, so, furthermore* and so on. For example,

Find a good camping ground and pitch your tent before dark.

While basic commands often require a simple and/or compound sentence structure, this task asked students to elaborate on their instructions. Sentences that effectively instruct and elaborate often require complex sentence structures. For example, sentences often begin with a conditional clause. For example,

In case you have an emergency (conditional subordinate clause) you should carry emergency supplies (main clause).

Instructions that provide reasons often follow the command with a causal subordinate clause. For example,

> Take a torch (main clause) *so you can see at night* (causal subordinate clause).

There are degrees or levels of complexity or subordination. For example, a subordinate clause can have another subordinate clause attached to it. This type of complexity is where one clause or unit of information is dependent on another clause for it to make complete sense. For example, in the following sentence, the first and second subordinate clauses are dependent on the main clause to make complete sense.

> *In order to keep warm* (conditional non-finite subordinate clause) *when you are camping overnight* (temporal subordinate clause) you should take a warm sleeping bag (main clause).

Another level of complexity is called embedding (as discussed in Chapter 2). This is where a clause is located within the structure of another clause or embedded within another clause. Adjectival clauses are said to be embedded because they do not have a dependent relationship with another clause (as in the preceding example), but instead add information to the subject or object of another clause. For example,

> A sleeping bag *that is down-filled* (embedded adjectival clause post-modifying the subject of the main clause [sleeping bag]) is best for warmth (main clause).

- Conduct a simple clause analysis exercise with the class. For example, display a non-procedural instruction for the class such as the following and with the class identify each clause and say whether it is a main/coordinate clause, a subordinate clause or an embedded/adjectival clause. Introduce the following tests to help with the identification.

  - If the clause can stand on its own and make complete sense it is a main or coordinating clause.
  - If the clause depends on a main clause for it to make complete sense it could be a subordinate clause or an embedded adjectival clause.
  - If the clause adds extra information to the subject or object of another clause then it is an embedded adjectival clause. For example,

Remember to take enough food (main clause) so you will not get hungry (subordinate clause). A map is essential (main clause) if you lose your way (subordinate adverbial clause) and will indicate the best route to take (coordinate clause).

Camping can be very dangerous (main clause) and can be miserable (coordinate clause) if there is a sudden change in the weather (subordinate clause). A good energy source of food is dried fruit (main clause). It also has sugar and vitamins (main clause) which replenish energy supplies (embedded adjectival clause).

- Provide the class with a similar non-procedural instruction and have them individually or in groups conduct a similar clause analysis. This is quite a complex activity and needs to be scaffolded carefully.

CHAPTER 7

THE GENRE
OF ARGUING

The genre of arguing is an important and influential language process, essential for dealing with many aspects of school knowledge and effective social participation. It is a process that involves reasoning, evaluation and persuasion.

In the past the skill of writing an effective argument was generally taught in the later years of school when the most common form of written argument, the essay, tends to dominate school writing. However, more recently, state syllabus documents appear to be challenging this notion. They acknowledge that the genre of arguing is a fundamental language process for teaching/learning in the learning areas in the infants and primary years. Each time a child is asked to:

- give an opinion of a story
- write about a topical issue, or
- give reasons for a viewpoint

he or she must employ the genre of arguing.

While students in the K-6 years may not have developed the cognitive skills to produce the type of essay required in the study of subjects at a secondary level, they do know how to express their opinion and to give reasons for a particular point of view. Comments such as 'I didn't like that, it was scary' and 'I liked that book because it was funny' are in fact early examples of argument and provide the foundation for developing the genre in its written form.

From their very early years, children are learning the rudimentaries of the complex grammar of argument. Together with the ability to formulate an opinion, they have grasped the basics of indicating causality in using words like 'because' when stating reasons for their viewpoint. They seem similarly equipped with the grammatical resources used to persuade. Children soon learn that 'Could I have a drink, please?' or 'I really need that, Mummy' will be more successful than simply saying, 'Give me that!'

The resources used in the genre of arguing, at least in speech, are therefore very much a part of a child's everyday life. Through interaction with adults and peers at home and school, they become quite proficient at delivering extremely effective spoken arguments. The aim here, therefore, is to tap into this proficiency in spoken arguments so that students can apply these skills to the written forms of this genre.

THE GRAMMATICAL FEATURES OF ARGUING

- Mental verbs are used when expressing opinions; for example,

  I *like* Girlfriend.
  We *believe* teachers shouldn't stop children from eating junk food.

- Connectives are used in arguing to maintain logical relations and to link points.

  - Temporal connectives are often used to order propositions in the preview or at other stages in a more complex argument; for example,

    There are a number of reasons why smoking shouldn't be allowed in restaurants. *Firstly*, many people can suffer from passive smoking and *secondly* it can aggravate asthma.

- Causal conditional connectives are used to link points in the argument; for example,

They die *because* the oil stops them from breathing.

- Comparative connectives are used to introduce counterpoints; for example,

However, others think we should have junk food.
On the other hand, packaging can have many disadvantages.

- Connectives can also exemplify and show results and are generally used in concluding statements to finalise arguments; for example,

Consequently, smoking shouldn't be allowed in restaurants.
Therefore we should change the Australian flag.

• Movement from personal to impersonal voice.

- The personal voice is used to indicate a subjective opinion such as through the first person pronoun *I*, or through the use of the second person pronoun *you*; for example,

I think we should change our flag.
You shouldn't drop rubbish.

- The impersonal voice is used to indicate an objective opinion, such as through the use of absolute statements or modalised statements; for example,

Packaging *is* essential in preserving and transporting products.
It *could* be argued that …

• Modality is used in arguing to position the writer and reader. It can be expressed in a number of ways; for example, through:

You *should* put rubbish in the bin.	Modal auxiliaries
I *think* children should go to school.	Mental verbs
It *will* make your class room look yucky.	Temporal auxiliaries

- Nominalisations are used in argument to allow the writer to condense information and deal with abstract issues. The process of nominalisation can also have the effect of removing agency.

Junk food can make people sick. / Junk food can cause *sickness*. This is the best way of using machines that people have today. / This is the best *application* of modern *technology*.

STRUCTURE OF ARGUMENTS

Depending on the purpose and particular context, the genre of arguing can take on different textual forms. Very often in the texts of younger students, and indeed with texts in general, more than one genre is used in the production of a text. Texts more often than not are multi-generic; that is, they draw upon a range of genres. This is the case in the text below, which is a mixture of arguing and describing.

Why I Like Girlfriend

I like Girlfriend because I think they sing well and they put a lot of expression into their songs.

Girlfriend wear groovy clothes. My favourite singer from Girlfriend is Melanie but Lorinda sings the best songs. My favourite songs are All or Nothing and Saving It Up. Girlfriend are good to dance to.

Year 3

This text, a young girl's opinion of the pop group Girlfriend, is generically an argument. The writer starts with the proposition, 'I like Girlfriend', which is then supported with points about the group's singing ability. Having said this, the remainder of the text is very much a description of the group's clothes and the writer's favourite singers and songs.

While the writer has quite successfully indicated her opinion of the group and given reasons for her viewpoint, she has drawn upon the more concrete generic resources of describing to complete this task.

A writer more proficient in this genre may have more clearly established causal links between liking the group and points about their clothes, individual singers and songs, thereby writing a more effective and persuasive argument. The text, however, demonstrates the writer's readiness for further developing her skills in writing argument, as well as the multi-generic nature of many texts.

EARLY ARGUMENTS

What clearly distinguishes the 'Girlfriend' text as an argument is its opening statement:

> I like Girlfriend because I think they sing well and they put a lot of expression into their songs.

This sentence contains the key structural features of argument (in all its textual forms); namely, a point or proposition followed by an elaboration. In teaching the genre of arguing to young writers, it is useful to begin at this point. Discussing students' opinions on issues and asking them why they think this way can be the first steps in developing the skills of argument. The sentences in the following text record Year 1 students' first attempts at argument in the school context.

I like the simsins	bekos they make me lafe.
Point/Proposition	*Elaboration*
We must line up for the tukshop	so we all get a turn.
Point/Proposition	*Elaboration*
Kids shud not drop paper	because it makes the playground messy.
Point/Proposition	*Elaboration*

Year 1

At this stage of development, written arguments often resemble explanations. This is because arguments and explanations of *why* both deal with causality. The distinguishing feature, however, is that an argument is primarily concerned with opinion and persuasion, whereas the purpose of explanation is to outline a process which may involve some level of interpretation (see Chapter 5).

EXPOSITIONS

In school, written arguments tend to focus on two main types: exposition and discussion. In teaching this genre, therefore, it is advisable to begin with exposition, a text type which clearly focuses students on the purpose of argument; that is, putting forward a viewpoint and providing evidence to support it.

Transporting Oil

I think we should protect our environment by transporting oil more safely.

Ships can spill oil and it can make a slick and fish and animals and birds can die. They die because the oil stops them from breathing.

This is why we should transport oil safely.

Year 2

This text is an example of a simple exposition. It can be structurally annotated, as follows:

Transporting Oil

I think we should protect our environment by transporting oil more safely.		Thesis
Ships can spill oil and it can make a slick and fish and animals and birds can die.	Point	Argument
They die because the oil stops them from breathing.	Elaboration	
This is why we should transport oil safely.		Conclusion

This text begins with a clearly stated thesis or major proposition; that is, 'I think we should protect our environment by transporting oil more safely.' Unlike the 'Girlfriend' text, the thesis here is clearly delineated. It is not accompanied by elaboration or any supporting statement in the same sentence, which is generally the pattern with early writers.

The thesis is followed by the argument stage. With texts produced by early writers, this may comprise only one point and elaboration. In many cases this is contained in the one sentence. As students develop in writing arguments, this stage becomes more complex. In essence, it is the 'core' of the argument. The points may increase in number, along with the degree of detail in the elaboration. The ordering of the points or the logic is of primary importance to the effectiveness of the argument. Quite often, more mature writers will include a counterpoint at this stage as a rhetorical device to position the reader.

The final stage of the exposition is the concluding statement where the thesis is reiterated, quite often literally in the texts of younger writers. In more complex texts, a summary is also given at this point.

Each of these stages has been clearly signalled by a new paragraph. It is useful to encourage students to organise their texts in paragraphs so as to highlight the different generic stages of the exposition.

Further development in writing expositions is evident in the following Year 5:

School

I think children should go to school. It is a place where they can learn, make friends and have fun.		Thesis
If they don't go to school children may never learn to read and write.	Point	Argument
This means that they might not get a good job or any job at all.	Elaboration	
At school children can learn about lots of different things like maths, science, famous people and different countries.	Point	Argument
At school you can also play sport and go on excursions to visit interesting places.	Elaboration	
That's why children should go to school.		Conclusion

Year 5

The thesis stage in this text is more complex than the argument of the Year 2 text, for example. It not only includes the statement of the thesis, 'I think children should go to school', but also a preview of points to be covered.

In the exposition by the Year 2 student, a preview to accompany the thesis is not necessary. However, as students develop their skills in writing arguments and begin to produce longer texts, the preview performs the very important function of allowing the writer to organise his or her thoughts and to prepare and position the reader for the argument to follow.

The argument stage in this text comprises a number of points that have each been elaborated upon. To some extent they have been placed in the order established by the preview. The exposition concludes with a reiteration of the thesis.

When students feel comfortable with the structural features of exposition they are more adequately prepared to tackle another text type of the genre of arguing: discussion.

DISCUSSIONS

While the purpose of an exposition is to present one viewpoint, a discussion is a more sophisticated argument as it involves the consideration of an issue from a number of perspectives. Discussions of early writers, however, are generally confined to statements for and against.

Getting a Dog – First Draft

My Dad wants to get a dog and Mum doesn't.	Statement of issue
Mum thinks they cost too much but Dad thinks they are fun to play with.	Arguments for and against
I think Dad is right that we should get a dog.	Recommendation

Year 3

Getting a Dog – Edited Copy

My Mum and Dad don't agree about getting a dog.	Statement of issue
Mum thinks they cost too much money because they have to go to the vet and they eat a lot of dog food.	Arguments against
Dad thinks they can be a good friend because you can go on walks together and play games.	Arguments for
I think Dad is right that we should get a dog.	Recommendation

The above annotations indicate the structural differences between discussions and expositions. Discussions use a *statement of issue* to indicate to the reader that there are at least two viewpoints on the issue under consideration. Compare this to the structure of expositions, which simply start with a thesis that puts forward a single proposition. Although not shown in this text, a discussion may include a preview of the points both for and against at the end of this stage.

Following the introductory paragraph, there are arguments for and against. In the edited version, both arguments include an elaboration. The number of points and the degree of elaboration depends to a large extent on the level of understanding and maturity of the writer.

In the first draft of 'Getting a Dog', the student simply includes a point both for and against in the one sentence. In the edited copy, each point is given its own sentence, one for and one against, both of which provide an elaboration signalled by the causal connective *because*.

The discussion concludes with a recommendation stage that states the viewpoint of the writer and summarises the evidence presented. A discussion is much more than a commentary on opposing viewpoints. In considering the 'pros' and 'cons' of a topic, a conclusion must be arrived at based on the evidence presented. The grammar of arguing allows the writer to guide the reader in drawing the appropriate conclusion. The annotated version of a Year 5 text below shows some development in writing discussion. The issue has been stated in the opening paragraph with some elaboration. The arguments for and against are also much more detailed, with the number of points and elaboration increased in each paragraph. While a summary of points is not included in the final paragraph, the recommendation is strengthened by being reiterated.

Junk Food

Year 5 at our school have been discussing whether or not we should have junk food at school.	Statement of issue	Issue
Some of the class think that we should have junk food but the others don't think so.	Preview	
Some kids think that we shouldn't have junk food	Point	
because you wouldn't grow up to be healthy and strong.	Elaboration	
Also junk food sometimes causes sickness to children	Point	Arguments against
if they eat too much of it.	Elaboration	
Junk food could rot teeth.		
Also when children buy junk food they throw their rubbish on the ground.	Point	
However, others think we should have junk food	Point	
because if there wasn't the children wouldn't go to the canteen and buy anything.	Elaboration	
Children enjoy junk food and so do many teachers.	Point	Arguments for
If parents allow children to eat junk food how could a school ban it?	Elaboration	
Our class thinks junk food should not be banned from school.	Summary	Recommendation
We believe that teachers shouldn't stop children from eating junk food.	Conclusion	

GRAMMAR OF ARGUING

While the language processes of describing and explaining basically represent the world in an objective fashion, arguing is about interpreting the world and persuading an audience of the validity of this interpretation. For this reason, the genre of arguing has developed a grammar that aims to:

- produce logical and coherent texts
- position both the writer and reader.

The first of these is achieved, to some extent, by the generic structure of an argument; that is, the ordering of the component parts of the text. However, it is reinforced by the grammar through the cohesive devices of connectives, reference and theme.

By positioning, we mean the way that writers rhetorically position readers into adopting particular ways of reading a text, or that they read texts in one way and not others. Some grammatical features are useful in this regard: resources such as modality, voice and, to some degree, nominalisation. It is the harnessing of these aspects of the grammar, to present a more objective argument, that presents a challenge for early writers.

Writing in the first years of school is very much like a transcription of speech. Early attempts at written arguments either barely acknowledge an audience, as in 'I think our canteen should sell junk food'; or conversely, address them directly, 'You shouldn't smoke because it is bad for you.' Concepts such as addressing a distant or intangible audience, and the associated subtleties of positioning, are not a feature of written arguments until the later years of primary and early junior secondary. The grammar of arguing, as with the grammatical resources already examined, therefore needs to be approached developmentally.

COMMONSENSE ARGUMENTS

The following texts demonstrate how students develop greater competence in using the grammar of arguing. They have been annotated to indicate some of the key grammatical features of the genre:

> Mental verbs – *italics*
> Modality – **bold**
> Connectives – <u>underlined</u>

The Simpsons

I *like* the Simpsons <u>because</u> they make me laugh.

Year 1

Although an early example of arguing, the text above uses some of the key grammatical features of the genre. The writer expresses her opinion by using the mental verb, *like*, and formalises the link between the point and elaboration with the causal connective *because*. The first person pronoun *I* signals the writer is using the personal voice to present this simple statement of taste.

Dropping Rubbish

You **shouldn't** drop rubbish at school <u>because</u> it will look very untidy.

<u>When</u> visitors come they will *think* it looks messy <u>and</u> they **will think** the children at this school are grubs. It **will** make your class room look yucky.

It **will** make birds, rats and mice come <u>and</u> eat the food scraps <u>and</u> the children **might** get a disease from the food going rotten in the playground.

You **should** put the rubbish in the bin to keep the playground clean.

Year 2

This text also makes use of the personal voice. However, in this example, the writer more directly addresses the reader through the use of the second person pronoun *you*. For this reason, the thesis and concluding statement read very much like instructions. In referring to the views of the visitors to the school, the writer uses the mental verb *think*. It is also interesting to note the number of action verbs in the text: *drop, make, come, eat*. This concrete use of language is characteristic of early writers of argument. It is generally not until upper primary that students begin to abstract their language by nominalising these verbs not processed.

The positioning of the reader is achieved through the use of modalities of both obligation (*shouldn't*) and probability (*will*). At this stage of development, the writer is unaware of the effectiveness of distancing herself from a point of view by using modalities of less obligation and probability. A less demonstrative stance in arguing often proves to be more successful. The logical relations in the text are established through the causal and additional connectives, *because* and *and*.

EXPOSITIONS

Changing the Flag

There are a couple of reasons why I *think* we **should** change the Australian flag. <u>Firstly</u> Australia is made up of people from lots of different countries. <u>Also</u> the flag we have doesn't show the Aborigines.

The Australian flag is made up of the Southern Cross and the Union Jack. The Union Jack is from England. Australia has people from lots of different countries not just England. This **should** be shown in our flag.

The Aborigines were the first people in Australia. The flag of Australia *needs* to show them too. These are the reasons why I *think* we **should** change our flag.

Year 4

While the writer opens and closes this exposition using the personal voice, *I think*, the remainder of the text is more objectively expressed, primarily through a series of absolute statements. She has ordered the points in the preview of her thesis by using the temporal connectives *firstly* and the additional connectives *also*. This is a common technique, which while cliched, can be useful when first teaching students how to write a preview to their thesis.

There appears to be an absence of either causal or additional connectives in this text. The logical relations between points are, rather, understood and achieved quite simply in the ordering of propositions.

The writer has used the mental verb *think* to modalise her thesis, but chooses the stronger mental verb *need*, and the modal auxiliary *should*, to demonstrate the strength of her convictions.

Sewage Pollution

I *think* the pollution on Sydney's beaches lately has been gross. The brown, sludgy, oily pollution floating around on the water has made swimming dangerous. This brown sewage contains chemicals which cause all sorts of infections and **can** make people very sick.

My solution to the matter is to buy a machine which turns sewage into useful products such as car fuel and fertilizers. This is the best application of modern technology for getting rid of this waste product. <u>Already</u> other countries have taken the upper hand and purchased one of these machines and they say it **can** even make money for their governments.

I personally *think* that no price is too high to save our beaches and I *know* a lot of you will *agree* with me.

Year 6

This text, as well as being a well-structured argument, also demonstrates some interesting grammatical features. The text begins and ends with personal opinion, *I think,* although the middle paragraph in particular shows an impressive range of objective rhetorical strategies. It is around about this age (Year 6) that students begin to employ abstract forms of language such as nominalisations — *application,* and metaphor — *other countries have taken the upper hand.*

TEACHING THE GENRE OF ARGUING

TARGET GROUP: YEARS 5/6

THE CONTEXT FOR ARGUMENTS/LINKS WITH CONCRETE EXPERIENCE

The genre of arguing is a language process central to dealing with content from across all of the learning areas of the curriculum. In the initial stages of teaching a topic, however, it is necessary to access content through the genres of describing and explaining. Issues that arise once students have a thorough knowledge of the field in which they are working may then be best treated through the genre of arguing.

To be meaningful and most effective, the teaching of language needs to be contextually based. In other words, a unit of work should not simply be about teaching a genre, or a specific text type, but teaching language processes through the content under focus. As teachers we need to think carefully about the connections between content and language, especially when developing language activities for our students.

In the integrated units of work which K–6 teachers develop for their students, literature is often used as a stimulus. As much of the fiction which even very young students read today has themes which highlight topical social issues, argument can be very effectively, and enjoyably, taught by examining these issues. The stimulus for the following teaching ideas is Robin Klein's *Junk Castle.* There are many books that could be approached in a similar way.

- When first reading and examining the text, a number of literature-based activities could be undertaken; for example,
    - shared reading
    - story frames
    - plot relationship charts
    - story maps
    - prediction charts
    - character profiles
    - character maps.

THE PURPOSE OF ARGUMENTS

- After students have a thorough knowledge of the text, conduct a brainstorming session framed by the following focus questions:
    - What is an issue?
    - What is the major issue in *Junk Castle*? – that is, an issue of kids' rights? Should the children's playhouse, Junk Castle, be removed from the local reserve?

- Broaden the discussion by asking students to compile a list of important issues at school; for example,
    - Should litter be dropped in the playground?
    - Should junk food be sold at the canteen?
    - Is more play equipment needed in the playground?
    - Should sport be compulsory?

Framing these issues as questions indicates to students that people may have different opinions about these issues.

- Focus on one of these issues and devise a class survey which can be administered to teachers and other students or kept solely as a class activity. Collate the results to determine the majority view. A questionnaire could also be designed and administered to determine why people hold particular views about an issue.

- With reference to the text, ask students how people express their viewpoint about an issue; for example, discussions, letters to newspapers, talk-back radio and TV.

These activities help focus students on the purpose of argument. They also serve as a more concrete introduction to developing an understanding of quite abstract concepts such as issues, opinions and propositions.

- Ask students to bring a variety of newspapers to school, and in groups examine the letters to the editor. Local newspapers are often more useful for this activity, as the issues that are dealt with are less difficult. Ask groups to choose two or three letters and to record the issue and opinion expressed in each; for example,

> *Issue*
> This letter is about after-school care.
>
> *Opinion*
> The writer thinks there should be after-school care at her son's school.
>
> *Issue*
> This letter is about trees in the local area.
>
> *Opinion*
> This writer thinks there should be more plantings of trees by the Council.

For younger students, this activity could be undertaken on a class basis, with the teacher providing greater assistance with reading and recording information.

- Have groups report back to the class with their results. Begin to discuss the nature of argument as a written form. Compare and contrast with other text types; for example, stories, recipes, reports and descriptions. Consider the different purpose of each text. Begin more explicitly to model the structure of an exposition. Using an OHP, display the letter to the editor from one of the characters in *Junk Castle*.

Mr Drake's letter to the Editor of the *Meldrum Gazette*

Sir,

Are you aware that a pile of rubbish and junk has been dumped recently in the Beatrice Binker Reserve? It constitutes a health hazard and a complete lack of civic pride. Something should be done about it immediately. The Beatrice Binker Reserve is a memorial park, and the Council should see that it is kept impeccably tidy at all times. I wish to see this abhorrence removed immediately.

Henry Drake, rate-payer

R. Klein (1983) *Junk Castle*, Melbourne, Oxford University Press, p. 32.

- Ask students questions which focus on purpose and highlight aspects of the structure:

  - What is the issue in Mr Drake's letter?
  - What is Mr Drake's viewpoint?
  - Where in the letter is the reader told this?
  - Why do you think he gives his view at this point?
  - What does he do next?
  - How many points does he make in his letter?
  - Does he explain his points?
  - How does he finish his letter?
  - In what way is it similar to his opening sentence?
  - If Mr Drake used paragraphs in his letter, where would they be?

- Use student responses to these questions to draw an outline, or scaffold, of an exposition for the class; for example,

  - Viewpoint
  - Point (1) and explanation
  - Point (2) and explanation
  - Concluding statement/Viewpoint repeated.

THE STRUCTURE OF ARGUMENTS

- Discuss each stage of the exposition and begin to use the generic terms with students.

  - Thesis
  - Point/Elaboration
  - Reiteration of the thesis.

- Ask the class to provide assistance in annotating Mr Drake's letter using the above terms. Discuss the effectiveness of his argument. Pay particular attention to his thesis. Discuss why he has constructed it as a question. What is the effect of doing this?

- Have students return to their original set of letters and in groups investigate if each has a thesis, points and elaboration, and a concluding statement where the thesis is repeated. Ask each group to present their results.

- Once students are familiar with the generic structure of an exposition provide them with a scaffold, as below, and have them draft a letter to the editor of the *Meldrum Gazette* supporting the Junk Castle in the Beatrice Binker Reserve.

Dear Sir or Madam	
	Thesis
	Point Argument Elaboration
	Point Argument Elaboration
	Conclusion
Signed _____ Date _____	

- Compare and contrast student responses, in terms of structure, to reinforce the generic stages of an exposition. This activity could alternatively be undertaken as a peer editing exercise.

THE GRAMMAR OF ARGUMENTS

Even in the very early years of school, students have little difficulty in understanding the structural features of argument. However, many of the grammatical features, as outlined on pp. 188–9, are best explicitly examined by students in mid to late primary. Grammatical features such as nouns and verbs are better understood through the more concrete genres of describing and explaining. However, as an introduction to the grammar of arguing, connectives and mental verbs are a good place to start.

CONNECTIVES

- Begin to examine students' drafts of their letter to the *Meldrum Gazette*. Take a sample of these texts and record the argument stage of each text on the board. Typical responses might include:

- The Junk Castle in the Beatrice Binker Reserve should not be removed because children in the area need a place to play.
- The Junk Castle isn't hurting anyone so it should be allowed to stay in the reserve.

• Draw students' attention to the words that link the point and elaboration. Discuss the function of these words in the sentence. Compile a list of these causal and additional connectives with students and ask them to identify these words in their own drafts. Encourage students to edit their drafts by asking the following questions:

- Have you only used 'because'?
- Are there other connectives that could do the same job?

IDENTIFYING VERBS

• Ask students also to identify the verbs in their draft and to record them on a grid under the headings of action, mental, and relational verbs.

• Investigate when students have used mental verbs.
- How many students have a mental verb in their thesis and in the reiteration of their thesis?
- Why might a mental verb be used in these stages of the text?
- Have they used mental verbs in other stages of their text?

• As an introduction to the notion of personal voice, record some of these responses on the board; for example,

- I think that Mr Drake is wrong in calling the playhouse in the local reserve an abhorrence.
- I believe the local kids should be congratulated for building the castle in the Beatrice Binker Reserve.

• Ask students for other opening sentences which do not use a mental verb and record these responses in a separate list. These examples might include:

- You shouldn't remove the Junk Castle from the Beatrice Binker Reserve because kids need somewhere to play.
- You shouldn't listen to angry old men who want to spoil children's fun, even if he is a ratepayer.

PERSONAL VOICE

- Responses which don't make use of the second person pronoun *you* should be recorded in a third list. These responses might include:

  - The local children's playhouse should not be removed from the local reserve.
  - Mr Drake's letter which says there is a pile of rubbish in the Beatrice Binker Reserve is wrong.

- Ask students to identify the personal pronouns in each group of sentences.

  Group 1   'I' (First person singular)
  Group 2   'You' (Second person)
  Group 3   No personal pronouns used.

- Discuss the use of voice in each of the different opening sentences by posing the following questions:

  - Why is the first person pronoun *I* used in the first group of sentences? Explain that the writer is giving his or her personal viewpoint. This is called the writer's voice or personal voice.
  - In what way are the first and second set of sentences different?

- Focus discussion on the use of the second person pronoun, *You*.

  - Who is the *You* in these sentences? Explain to students that the *You* is the reader.
  - Why does the writer start the sentence this way? Explain that the writer is speaking directly to the reader. This is a different example of personal voice.
  - What other types of writing do these sentences sound like? Explain how these sentences sound very much like instructions. Discuss other examples.
  - Is the writer's voice obvious in the third set of sentences? Explain that the writer's voice is not obvious and that this is called impersonal voice.
  - How is the audience addressed in these sentences?
  - In what way is the use of personal and impersonal voice different?
  - Why is it important to consider how the audience is addressed when writing an argument?

- Conduct exercises on moving from the personal to the impersonal voice. Refer to the school issues discussed earlier in the unit outline; for example,

Personal	Impersonal
I think the school needs more playground equipment.	The school needs more playground equipment.
You shouldn't throw things in class.	Things shouldn't be thrown in class.

OBJECTIVE/SUBJECTIVE ARGUMENTS

- Ask students to consider the shift that has occurred in the grammar in moving from the personal to the impersonal voice by posing the following questions:

  - Which example sounds more like an opinion and which seems more like a fact?
  - Which sounds more authoritative or important?
  - Could the different forms be used for different audiences?
  - In what circumstances are the different forms more appropriate?

MODALITY

The grammatical resources of voice and modality are closely linked. Together they function as the key rhetorical devices of arguing, yet they can be examined from the earliest years of schooling. To begin an examination of modality, return to some of the students' opening 'I think' statements.

As well as indicating the personal voice of the writer, ask students what other effect the use of *I think* has on the statement. That is, it provides some qualification or modality. The writer is saying *I think* this, it is only my viewpoint and nobody else's. In certain circumstances this may be a more effective way of expressing opinion. The use of impersonal voice may be far too dogmatic. Remind students that arguing is not merely about presenting an argument, but also about convincing the writer of its worth.

- Examine other ways of qualifying or modalising statements with students. Write a proposition on the board; for example,

  - Running in the hall is dangerous.

- Ask students for ways they might modalise this statement and record their responses; for example,

  > Running in the hall could be dangerous.
  > Running in the hall might be dangerous.
  > It is possible that running in the hall is dangerous.
  > It is probable that running in the hall is dangerous.
  > Running in the hall is certainly dangerous.

- Ask students to consider the audience for each of these statements. Who would be more likely to use 'is' as opposed to 'might'?

The degree of modality could also be considered. Have students discuss whether a word is expressing low, medium or high modality, and record their responses on a class grid, as below:

Low	Medium	High
may	will	must
possibly	probably	certainly

Depending on the ability of students and the time available within a unit, students could also begin to identify the range of grammatical forms that express modality; for example,

Nouns	Auxiliary verbs	Adjectives	Adverbs
possibility	can	possible	possibly
	might		

- Return to Mr Drake's letter and discuss with students how he uses modality in his argument.

  > Sir,
  >
  > Are you aware that a pile of rubbish and junk has been dumped recently in the Beatrice Binker Reserve? It constitutes a health hazard and a **complete** lack of civic pride. Something **should** be done about it **immediately**. The Beatrice Binker Reserve is a memorial park, and the Council **should** see that it is kept **impeccably** tidy at all times. I **wish** to see this **abhorrence** removed **immediately**.
  >
  > Henry Drake, rate-payer

- Ask students to identify examples of modality in their own drafts.

NOMINALISATION

Nominalisation is a grammatical feature of the arguments of more mature writers in that it is essential for dealing with abstract knowledge. It begins to become evident in students' writing as early as mid to late primary.

The process of nominalising can also be taught to students as an editing strategy. A knowledge of nominalisation, and its effect on writing, can assist students in making the transition from a purely speech-oriented form of writing, which is heavily action, or verb based, to a more thing, or noun-based written construction.

- As a starting point for understanding nominalisation, ask students to refer to the action verbs they have already identified in their draft exposition. Compile a list of these verbs on the board and as a class exercise turn these processes (verbs) into things (nouns); for example,

  remove/removal
  need to play/recreation
  should be congratulated/congratulations
  building/construction

- Choose a couple of these verbs and ask students for the sentence in which they are found. Record these sentences on the board, and with the class rewrite the sentence using the noun form of the verb; for example,

  You shouldn't remove the Junk Castle from the Beatrice Binker Reserve because kids need somewhere to play.

  The removal of the Junk Castle from the Beatrice Binker Reserve would seriously impede local children's recreation.

  I believe the local kids should be congratulated for building the castle in the Beatrice Binker Reserve.

  Congratulations are due to the local kids for the construction of the castle in the Beatrice Binker Reserve.

- Discuss the effect of nominalising with students. Consider how nominalisation increases the number of relational verbs used in a text.

- Ask students to edit their draft expositions using the same process. Explain that they need not use all the noun forms, only those that they consider may improve their draft.

Depending on the ability level of students and the time available, consideration can be given to using a range of these grammatical editing strategies in completing the revision of the draft expositions. When final copies are completed, students' letters could be published in a class news sheet of letters to the editor of the *Meldrum Gazette*.

ASSESSING TEXTS USING THE GENRE OF ARGUING: AN EXPOSITION

The following writing task asked Year 6 students to write an article for the local newspaper arguing for the community to plant more trees in public spaces. The students were given three points outlining the benefits of tree planting and told the appropriate structural features of a written argument.

Task
Imagine that your local area does not have many trees. You have been asked to write to your local newspaper to convince people that it is a good idea to plant more trees. Write an argument to persuade people that this is a good idea.

Use these points to help you:

• good for the environment
• provide shade
• appearance – trees look good.

Hints

• Make sure that your writing is only about the topic – why people should plant more trees.
• You should write in sentences.
• You should pay attention to spelling and punctuation.
• You should finish your writing with a conclusion that sums up your arguments.
• Use your planning time to organise your main points.
• Remember to use the time at the end of the task to read and edit. Imagine that your local area does not have many trees.

The following are the assessment criteria used for assessing the task based on the appropriate generic structural and grammatical features described earlier in this chapter.

1 *Genre-based* criteria deal with the macro-level features of the text. This level covers the first set of criteria:

- does the text argue and/or persuade?
- is the theme of the writing consistent with the task?
- is the writing well organised and logical, and does it include a statement of thesis, arguments and a conclusion?
- does the writing use appropriate rhetorical, persuasive devices such as modality, rhetorical questions and refutation?
- does the writing use a range of effective language (vocabulary)
- is the argument written in first, second or third person?

2 *Textual language* criteria deal with the way that the text is held together, the way that sentences are structured and how sentences work with one another. This level covers the next set of criteria:

- does the text use a range of simple, compound and complex sentence structures?
- is the choice of tense appropriate and consistently maintained?
- is the text cohesive through the appropriate use of pronouns?
- does the text make appropriate use of a variety of connectives?

3 *Syntactical language* criteria deal with the internal structure of the sentences used. This level covers the next criteria:

- do the sentences have essential elements such as a main verb and do statements have the subject and main verb in the correct order?
- do the subject and main verb agree in person and number?
- are prepositions used appropriately?
- are articles always used correctly?
- is simple and complex punctuation correct?

4 *Spelling* deals with the way that individual words across the text are spelt. This level comprises the following criteria:

- are most high-frequency words spelt correctly?
- are most less frequently used words and words with common but not simple patterns spelt correctly?

- are most words with difficult or unusual patterns spelt correctly?
- are most challenging words appropriate to the task spelt correctly?
- are all challenging words appropriate to the task spelt correctly?

Plant More Trees

1 Currently in the community a debate is raging on
   based on Should we plant more trees. In the next three
   paragraphs I will state why we should plant more trees.
   Firstly planting trees is good for the environment
5 because trees provide oxegen which we breath in. We
   breath out carbon dioxide and trees breath in carbon dioxide.
   Secondly trees also provide shade for us. Say for
   example you were playing soccer at the park on a hot day,
   you forgot to a water botle and you were exhausted. You
10 could sit under the tree and cool down.
   Thirdly trees are good looking. Many tourists
   Come to Australia every year to see The Royal
   Botanic gardens so if we plant more trees we could
   probably make the second Royal Botanic gardens
15 in Strathfield!
       I think trees should be planted because if their
   are no trees we won't be able to live so thats why
   I think we should plant more trees.

Year 6

GENRE

GENRE AND THEME

The writing mainly argues, but there is too little depth in the arguments for the text to be persuasive. The theme is consistent and stays on the task.

TEXT STRUCTURE

The writing begins with a thesis and the arguments are supported by some elaboration. The conclusion reinforces the writer's position.

RHETORICAL DEVICES

There is a limited range of modalities (l. 2 *should*, l. 10 *could*, l. 13 *if*, l. 14 *probably*).

LANGUAGE

There is some use of <u>effective</u> vocabulary (l. 1 *currently, raging,* l. 9 *exhausted*).

VOICE

Third person is not used consistently; for example, first person is used (l. 3 *I,* l. 16 *I*) and second person (you) is used l. 8 and 9.

TEXTUAL LANGUAGE

SENTENCE STRUCTURE

Most simple and compound sentences are correct and there is one sentence with an embedded adjectival clause (l. 1) and one complex sentence is successfully structured (l. 4 *Firstly planting trees is good* …). However, most complex sentences are poorly structured (l. 7–9, l. 11–15, l. 16–18).

TENSE

Tense is generally consistent, although there is inappropriate use of tense in l. 13 *so if we plant[ed] more trees*).

PRONOUNS

Pronouns are used correctly throughout the text.

CONNECTIVES

There is a limited range of connectives (*Firstly, because, Secondly, Thirdly*).

SYNTACTICAL LANGUAGE

CLAUSE PATTERN

Sentences always have a main clause and all finite clauses have a subject and finite verb.

AGREEMENT

All verb forms agree with their subjects.

ARTICLES

All articles and plurals are correct.

PUNCTUATION

All sentence punctuation is correct, but there is inconsistent use of capitals (l. 6 *Carbon*, l. 13, 14 *g[G]ardens*) and contractions (l. 17 *that[']s*).

SPELLING

Most less frequently used words and words with common but not simple patterns are spelt correctly, but *bottle* is incorrectly spelt (l. 9), as are some other words with less common spellings: *oxegen* (l. 5) *breath* (l. 6).

SUMMARY

This text demonstrates a basic understanding of the genre by following the task and model. It demonstrates an elementary understanding of the structure for the genre. The writing argues but does not persuade, and there is only a limited use of rhetorical devices and persuasive language. The writing demonstrates a suitable level of sentence structure and syntax, although not all complex sentences are successful. Most less frequently used words are spelt correctly, although some difficult words are incorrect. Most sentence and simple punctuation is correct, although there are some basic errors in capitalisation and the use of apostrophes.

STRATEGIES TO MOVE STUDENTS FROM BASIC TO PERSUASIVE ARGUMENTS

Many of the strategies that could move this student from writing a basic to a more mature argument have been outlined in the teaching strategies earlier in this chapter. Here we focus specifically on whole-class activities that address persuasive language, voice, complex sentence structure and connectives, and key problems with this student's text.

PERSUASIVE LANGUAGE

The effective use of rhetorical language is the feature that makes an argument effective and persuasive. The following strategies are designed to assist students to develop their use of persuasive language in their arguments

- A useful way to explore the nature and impact of persuasive language is to investigate the language of advertising. Have students bring a variety of advertisements from magazines or newspapers to class that rely on the written rather than the visual text to sell a product. Prior to students examining the advertisements, make an OHT of the example below (or similar), display and discuss.

> **SUDSO**
> Smart people buy Sudso – The only dishwashing liquid that brings
> a guaranteed sparkle and shine to your dishes.
> Sudso also contains a clinically tested antibacterial agent
> to ensure your dishes are hygienically clean.
> BUY SUDSO!
> DON'T TAKE THE RISK WITH OTHER BRANDS!

- Ask students to consider the word and phrases which have been used to encourage them to buy the product; for example,

smart	adjective
only	adverb
a guaranteed sparkle and shine	noun phrase
a clinically tested antibacterial agent	noun phrase
(to) ensure	verb
hygienically	adverb
risk	noun

- Identify each grammatical category, as above, and discuss the particular effect of each; for example, reference to science, uniqueness and so on. Point out how affective language covers a range of grammatical categories, including the use of adjectives within noun phrases and adverbs to add meaning to verbs.

- Following this activity, in groups have students examine the advertisements they have brought to class identifying, categorising and pinpointing the effect of each example, as has been modelled in the example above. Have each group report back and discuss results.

- To conclude the activity have students write their own advertisements on a product of their choice using the appeal of affective language to sell the item.

PERSON

As our assessment indicates, this student shifts between first and second person throughout the text. If other students are experiencing similar difficulties with consistently maintaining third person throughout their expositions, it would be useful to employ the teaching strategies outlined earlier in this chapter on personal voice. In addition to these strategies, however, the following would be a useful class activity.

Once students are familiar with the terminology and pronouns used to indicate first, second and third person, briefly discuss why third person is more effective in written arguments such as expositions.

Use the assessment example here or another similar example and display on a board or OHP. As a class activity identify all personal pronouns and indicate whether they are first, second or third person.

Plant More Trees

Currently in the community a debate is raging on based on Should we plant more trees. In the next three paragraphs I will state why we should plant more trees.

Firstly planting trees is good for the environment because trees provide oxegen which we breath in. We breath out carbon dioxide and trees breath in carbon dioxide.

Secondly trees also provide shade for us. Say for example you were playing soccer at the park on a hot day, you forgot to a water botle and you were exhausted. You could sit under the tree and cool down.

Thirdly trees are good looking. Many tourists Come to Australia every year to see The Royal Botanic gardens so if we plant more trees we could probably make the second Royal Botanic gardens in Strathfield!

I think trees should be planted because if their are no trees we won't be able to live so thats why I think we should plant more trees.

First	Second	Third
we	you	
I	you	
we	you	
we	you	
we		
us		
we		
we		
I		
we		
I		

As a class activity jointly re-write the text replacing the first and second person pronouns where possible.

> Currently in the community a debate is raging on based on *whether to plant* more trees The next three paragraphs will argue why *planting more trees is the best thing to do.*
>
> Firstly planting trees is good for the environment because trees provide oxegen *for humans to breathe* as humans breathe out carbon dioxide and trees breathe it in.
>
> Secondly trees also provide shade. For example, <u>when</u> playing soccer at the park on a hot day, trees could provide shade and protection and when people become exhausted.
>
> Thirdly trees are good looking. Many tourists Come to Australia every year to see The Royal Botanic gardens so if more trees are planted there could be a need to make the second Royal Botanic gardens in Strathfield!
>
> Trees should be planted because if their are no trees people wouldn't be able to live so thats why more trees should be planted.

Finally, discuss why the re-written version is more effective in a written argument.

- it no longer sounds like a speech or debate

- it is more like what would be written in a newspaper article

- it is more objective because it no longer reads like it is only the opinion of one person

- it is more difficult to argue against because it no longer reads like it is the opinion of one person.

SENTENCE STRUCTURE

While aspects of writing complex sentences have already been discussed in Assessing Texts Using the Genre of Instructing, the information provided here focuses more specifically on the construction of the type of complex sentences typically used in written arguments.

- Complex sentences are sentences that contain two or more clauses, one of which must be a main or independent clause and the other or others are adverbial clauses that are dependent on the main clause for meaning. Students often have problems writing complex sentences because they fail to include a main clause in what they assume to be a sentence. To be successful at writing complex sentences, students need to be able to differentiate between main and subordinate or dependent clauses. To assist students in developing this understanding write a selection of complex sentences on the board as below:

1 [Although sweets taste good] they can be bad for you.

2 [Because of the high fat content of some types of junk food], it is best not to eat it too often.

3 [While sugar is important in a balanced diet], it is important to be aware of the sugar content of food and drink.

- Read the sentences aloud and ask students if each is a sentence. Following this, cover the subordinate clauses within the sentences, those not bracketed, and read aloud. Ask students if these could be sentences. If there appears to be disagreement ask students whether the information can stand on its own; that is, is it a complete unit of information? Next cover the main clauses and ask students if the subordinate clauses could be sentences. Once again, if there is disagreement ask if each clause can make complete sense on its own.

- After the class has reached consensus, explain that these examples are complex sentences. They contain two clauses but only one is a main clause and can function as a sentence in its own right. Return to the subordinate clauses and ask students which words signal that these clauses are subordinate to the main clause; that is, *although, while* and *because*. Point out that they are called 'subordinate conjunctions'.

- To conclude the activity have students write examples of complex sentences using the subordinate conjunctions on the board. Following this have students peer edit each other's work, circling the subordinate conjunctions and underlining the main clause. Pool results and review definitions of each grammatical term.

STRATEGIES TO IMPROVE THE USE OF CONNECTIVES

See page 49 for some examples of the types of connectives often used in arguments.

- *Temporal connectives* are often used to order propositions in the introduction or at other stages in a more complex argument; for example,

first	when	now
meanwhile	finally	next
lastly	afterwards	then
soon	previously	at once

- *Causal-conditional connectives* are used to link points in the argument; for example,

so	consequently	accordingly
despite this	moreover	hence
however	nevertheless	because
as a result of	therefore	stemmed from

- *Comparative connectives* are used to introduce counterpoints and refutation; for example,

however	whereas	on the other hand
on the contrary	rather	in spite of this
alternatively	differs from	instead

Comparative connectives are more often used in discussions than expositions.

- *Additive connectives* are used to add to and further develop the argument; for example,

also	but	and
in addition	besides	moreover
as well	while	whereas

- To focus students' attention on the different types of connectives and their use in writing arguments, divide the board in two. Begin by providing a definition of connectives as joining words and provide some examples. Brainstorm a list of connectives recording responses on one section of the board. Add to the list if a certain category is deficient. Next point out to students that these connectives have different functions. Divide the second section of the board into four columns with the headings: temporal connectives, causal connectives, comparative connectives and additive connectives.

- Have students categorise the brainstormed connectives and record their responses under the columns. Consider how some words may belong to more than one category. In other words, where they belong will depend on what they're doing in a particular sentence.

- After this, discuss the type of connectives used in different stages of an argument.

- To reinforce their different function, complete cloze exercises on connectives using argument texts. Also, have students assess the variety of conjunctions used in their own recent argument texts.

CHAPTER 8

THE GENRE
OF NARRATING

The genre of narrating or narrative is one of the most commonly read, though least understood of all the genres. Because narrative has been and continues to be such a popular genre, there is a belief that it is a genre that students 'pick up' and write 'naturally'. Story-writing therefore has been prominent as a means of naturally inducting students into the intricacies and idiosyncrasies of the English language.

The first point we would want to make, therefore, is that this genre, while being universally popular, is far from natural; nor is it easy to simply 'pick up' for a significant number of students. Why is it that some students are 'natural' story-writers while others never seem to 'pick it up'?

Narrative does not have, for example, a singular generic purpose as do some of the other genres. We cannot say that narrative is simply about entertaining a reading audience, although it generally always does so. Narrative also has a powerful social role beyond that of being a medium for entertainment. Narrative is also a powerful medium for changing social opinions and attitudes. Think about the way that some soap operas and television dramas use narrative to raise topical social issues and present their complexities and different perspectives in ways that are not possible in news reports and current affairs programs.

Narrative is also a 'big' or macro genre in that it can easily accommodate one or more of the other genres and still remain dominant. Countless books have been written about narrative and it is outside of the scope of this chapter to deal with anything more than the types of narrative that primary school-age students are expected to write. Our aim, therefore, is to provide a sound basis for teaching the basic techniques of narrative writing so that students may proceed beyond primary education to develop, and even break out of, some of the generic boundaries established here.

GRAMMATICAL FEATURES OF NARRATING

- When sequencing people and events in time and space, narrating typically uses:

  - action verbs; for example,

    One day the man and his son *went collecting* fire-wood. They *saw* a golden tree. They *went* slowly over to the tree. When they *got* closer to the tree they *heard* a voice *coming* from the tree.

  - temporal connectives; for example,

    We *then* looked at some games and equipment. *After* lunch we walked up to the *Sydney Morning Herald* and saw how they make papers. *After* that we caught the train back to Marrickville.

- Recounts and stories are typically written in the past tense unless quoting direct speech; for example,

  They *were* poor because their pig *ate* them out of house and home and he *didn't share* with the other animals. His name *was* Bob. 'You *should go* on a diet' *said* Clarabelle.

- In action sequences, mainly action verbs (bold) are used, while in reflections/evaluations, mental verbs (italicised) predominate; for example,

> Bells **were ringing**, sirens **screeching** and people **were running** everywhere.
> Maria *didn't know* what to do next. She *thought* about her mother and *wondered* what was in her head.

- Narratives often use action verbs metaphorically to create effective images; for example,

> It was a terrible argument. Words were *flying* everywhere.

- Narratives often use rhythm and repetition to create particular effects; for example,

> *Riding. Riding.* The boy went *riding* across the wintery moor, far away from the strife of his unhappy home.

- Play with sentence structure is another common feature of narratives. Often sentences comprising one word or a short phrase are used to create poignant effects; for example,

> *Anger, Silence. As the vengeful brother prowls the streets.*

> Rose slowly opened the old wooden door. *Dark.* There was nothing but black.

NOTE As mentioned, narrating is a macro genre. It incorporates other genres; in particular, describing. Refer to the grammatical features of describing on pp.98–100 for an account of the descriptive devices often employed in narrative.

BASIC STRUCTURE OF NARRATIVES

Formally, narrative sequences people/characters in time and space. In its most basic form, in text types such as recounting and retelling, the genre does little more than simply sequence. A key characteristic for all text types in the genre, however, is the requirement to orient or introduce the reader/listener to the people, time and place in the story. The structure of narrative is generally more complex than the orientation and sequencing typical of recounting. Stories, for example, bring a rather complex dimension into play. More than simply sequencing a series of events, stories use the sequence to set up one or more complexities or problems. It is this problem making that usually draws the reader into the narrative, provided that the reader can empathise with the characters. This problem part of the narrative must eventually find some way of being resolved, otherwise we are left with very frustrated or angry readers. Good problem-solving skills are a necessary part of writing successful narratives, and this is the stage that most young writers find the most difficult. Think about how many times you have read '… and then I woke up and it was only a dream' or, '… and then the bell went and we all went into school'.

In our approach to *genre, text* and *grammar*, we would see the structure of narrative as an ideal starting point for teaching narrative writing. However, it is only that a starting point − as control of the structure alone does not necessarily mean that students will be able to write an interesting narrative.

RECOUNTS

ORIENTATION

Recounts are the simplest text type in this genre. Formally, recounts are sequential texts that do little more than sequence a series of events. Every story, no matter how simple, needs an orientation. Indeed, it is impossible to tell a story unless we see that there are characters set up in a particular time and place, although many postmodern narratives play with these conventions. There are different ways of teaching this stage of narrative writing; for example,

- characters, time, place
- who, what, where, when and so on.

In simple recounts the orientation stage need only be a sentence, as in the following example.

> *On Wednesday we went camping here at school.* We had chicken and chips at camp. We sung songs around the camp fire and I stayed the night.
>
> Year 1

SEQUENCE OF EVENTS

As well as providing an orientation, the above recount sequences three events: eating dinner, singing songs and staying the night. The next recount, of a class excursion, would be familiar to most teachers. The orientation paragraph is typical of this type of recount. The sequence of events stage, however, is more complex than the previous recount. Here the student provides a record of all the important activities that happened on the excursion.

Yesterday Year 5/6 went on an excursion to the Power House Museum.	Orientation
When everyone arrived at school we walked to Marrickville station. Our class caught the 9.30 train to Central station. When we got off at Central we walked through the Devonshire St tunnel to Harris St. We walked in the museum and we saw some slides and a movie. The movie was about communication and it was called Get The Message. We then looked at some games and equipment. After lunch we walked up to the Sydney Morning Herald and saw how they make papers. After that we caught the train back to Marrickville.	Sequence of events

Year 5

SIMPLE NARRATIVES

Simple narratives or stories add a major dimension to the structure of a recount. Although narratives have many of the basic features of recounts, textually they set up a complexity of some sort that must be resolved. When students first attempt narratives, they find the orientation and complication stages fairly straight forward, as they are similar to the structure and grammar of recounts. The resolution stage, however, is another matter. In the following recount the writer has simply taken the 'they lived happily ever after' ending typical of fairy tales in order to solve the problem.

Once there was an old man. His wife had died and he had married again. The man had one son and his stepmother had a daughter.	Orientation
One day the man and his son went collecting fire-wood. They saw a golden tree. They went slowly over to the tree. When they got closer to the tree they heard a voice coming from the tree. This is what the tree said. Go north for one and a half miles. Ther you will find a fairy wearing a gold ring. You must take the ring and make a wish.	Sequence of events
They dun just as the fairy had said and they lived happy every after.	Resolution

Year 3

The complication stage of simple narratives needn't be a single problem or complexity. This stage can also include reflection on the problem and possible solutions. The following text by a Year 4 student outlines a simple story with a problem, a solution and finally a resolution.

A long time ago there was a barn with owners named Mr and Mrs Smith. They were poor and they only had a horse for riding, 2 sheep for wool,1 pig and a bull and a cow for milk.	Orientation
They were poor because their pig ate them out of house and home and he didn't share with the other animals. His name was Bob. 'You should go on a diet' said Clarabelle the horse. 'Oh be quiet, I'm not fat I've got big bones'. A few minutes later Bob was rolling around on the ground. 'I'm sick, I'm sick', he shouted. 'Help me, help me'. Mr and Mrs Smith ran down and called the vet. The vet came quickly and said quietly, 'If he eats like he has been eating he'll surely die'. 'Oh', groaned the pig.	Problem

Continued next page

Clarabelle overheard and said to the other animals, 'Our friend is dying, we've got to help him'. 'Yeh' said the other animals 'lets go'. They went up to Bob and said, 'We are going to get you in shape'. First they told him to eat only half of the food in the trof. Then they made him run up and down the hill and made him swim in the duck pond.	Solution
He did this every day for three long weeks and he got better and he thanked Clarabelle and Bob was never greedy again.	Resolution

Erin Year 4

In the latter part of this chapter we will see how this student developed her story from a thematic plan with the assistance of the generic structure. Here the theme being developed is that greed is a negative quality, and that it is better to be cooperative and to share. The field for this story is generic in the sense that she uses farmyard animals who display human attributes as the main characters.

FABLES

Fables are another useful narrative form for developing young writers' understanding of theme and narrative structure. In the text below the moral of 'One good turn deserves another' acts as a cohesive device for the structural elements of orientation, complication and resolution. The moral often assists students in the difficult process of resolving the complications they have introduced into their texts. Here, in writing this fable, the writer knows that his resolution must involve a good turn. The focus then shifts to deciding upon the characters and storyline in completing the text.

The Good Germs and the Bad Germs

Once upon a time in a sick man's body there lived an army of good germs and an army of bad germs. One day the bad germs caught the good germs and the good germs begged the bad germs to let them go. The bad germs decided to give the good germs a second chance and let them go. Then one day the sick man drank some purple medicine called Dimetapp. The bad germs got flooded and just at that moment the good germs thought of a spectacular idea. The good germs made a tastebud wall so the bad germs could climb out of the medicine. Moral – One good turn deserves another.

Declan Year 1

THEMATIC STRUCTURE

Somewhere between Years 4/5 and Years 8/9, students make major transformations in their use of written language. Storytelling is obviously closely related to spoken language, and provided that young children have been exposed to storytelling, they tend to incorporate the salient textual features into their written stories, all of which is evident in the texts above. As students develop in their use of language, however, they move out of the speech-like features of storytelling towards a more written form of narrative – a form that is more literary and poetic, and which uses the form of language to create complex and effective imagery.

In the following story by a Year 9 student, the generic structure of *orientation, complication* and *resolution* is no longer recognisable. Here the student has planned her story around themes and images, employing metaphors to enhance the imagery. The field is an urban ghetto developed through the metaphor of the jungle. The themes of mindless justice and revenge and the reduction of life to the 'law of the jungle' help to create the overall message of the meaninglessness of death, violence and revenge.

The Civilised World

Anger. Silence. As the vengeful brother prowls the streets. The rhythmic beat of skipping ropes. The hum and hiss of distant traffic. Determined footsteps, beating, beating. Inhuman thoughts in a numb body – trapped, waiting, ready to fire. He knows no law but the law of the jungle … do unto others, etc.

Innocence is the first victim of suburban war.

Searching, seeking, honing in on the victim. Slowly, silently moving in for the kill, he raises his gun. My sister – your brother. White eyes staring, afraid and searching.

Numbness.

BANG

The echoing silence of fighters and death. The calm after the storm and then the thunder of screams. Shock. Brave but timid they emerge from the concrete. Who, where, why and how?

Numb and naive, not knowing he stands there – waiting, watching and then he runs to the predators. Waiting, wanting, needing approval.

In his mind justice has been served.

Melinda, Year 9

Notice how the writer is attempting to use unconventional forms of writing to develop an effect. She experiments with techniques such as rhythm, repetition, alliteration and unusual punctuation to help build up images for her readers. In this story the images and themes take up a more dominant position than the plot.

GRAMMAR OF NARRATING

In a general sense, it is difficult to specify particular grammatical features as typical of narratives. Narratives, after all, can do almost anything with language. We can, however, look at some typical grammatical features; in particular, those used by early writers as their writing develops from the speech-like constructions of recounts towards the more abstract/metaphorical language of mature narrative writers.

RECOUNTS

Recounts, of all the written text types, most closely resemble the grammar of speech. As we have already seen, recounts basically sequence events temporally. We would therefore expect to see a predominance of action verbs (**bold**) and temporal connectives (*italicised*). For example:

Colonial Day

On Monday our school **held** a Colonial Day. People **dressed** as maids, farmers, soldiers, settlers, gold miners, school children and bush rangers. *First* we **did** the heal and toe pocker. *Then* 5R and 6B **performed** another dance. Then 2W **performed** another dance.

Then we all **went** inside until recess. During recess we **ate** bread with golden syrup on it. *After* morning tea we all **enjoyed** Greg Dimmock's performance. He **showed** us some musical instruments, toys and chains of convicts. He also **sang** old songs for us. *After* lunch we all **went** to the gold rush. Everyone in my class **found** gold. It was fun and everyone **enjoyed** it.

Year 3

SIMPLE NARRATIVES

One way of helping students to develop their writing skills in this genre, from recounting past experiences to developing ways of writing stories, is by having them retell stories they have read in class. In the following example, we can see how this young writer is still using the grammatical features of recounts, but has introduced dialogue (<u>underlined</u>) to help draw out the complexities of the story.

Enora and the Black Crane

A long time ago when the world was new lived a man called Enora. He and his family **lived** in a rainforest with fish fruit and lovely food. Enora and his family **would swim** in the river. *One day* Enora **saw** some colours in the sky. *One day* he **went** to a clearing and **saw** lyrebirds, parrotts and emus. Enora **went** back to the clearing again and **took** a long stick and **killed** a black crane with it. *All of a sudden* he **looked** at his hands and it **was covered** with feathers. He **tried to pull** them out but he **couldn't**. He **went** back to the rainforest and **told** his family all about it but they did not believe him. <u>I must go to the clearing one more time</u> he said to himself. *That night* he had a dream about the colours. **The next day** his hands and body **were covered** with feathers. *Then* he **went** back to the clearing. The birds **were waiting** for him. All the birds were different colours but Enora was just black.

Year 3

CREATIVE STORIES

Writing stories provides students with opportunities to 'play' with language and experiment with its potential. The following story by a Year 5 student uses the generic elements of a 'super-hero' story in an inventive way — in this case, to encourage children to brush their teeth. In an action-based story like this, you will notice that there are a lot of action verbs and that the sentences are short and rhythmical.

Supertoothbrush and his assistant Toothpaste

One day Supertoothbrush sat waiting for a call. Suddenly in ran Miss Bandaid with the phone. 'A call for you Brushy', she panted and rushed out, closing the door behind her. As STB answered the phone his assistant Toothpaste pulled open the door a bit and then slammed it shut because Miss Bandaid was listening.

The caller was Betty Lou. Her kids teeth were drastically turning yellow and green from Plaquey and his vicious gang.

STB and Powerful Toothpaste flew straight to Betty Lou's house and rushed to the toothbrush drawer and inside they went.

When it was bedtime, Tom (Betty's son) came in and began to brush his teeth with STB and Powerful Toothpaste and that was when the fight began.

First STB pushed away six of the vicious gang with his bristles. Then PTP whipped away six more. Together they made the vicious plaque gang disappear completely.

So brush your teeth every day and every night because you never know, they might be out there.

Laura, Year 5

The Civilised World

Anger. Silence. As the vengeful brother prowls the streets. The rhythmic beat of skipping ropes. The hum and hiss of distant traffic. Determined footsteps, *beating, beating*. Inhuman thoughts in a numb body – trapped, waiting, ready to fire. He knows no law but the law of the jungle... do unto others, etc.

Innocence is the first victim of suburban war.

Searching, seeking, honing in on the victim. *Slowly, silently* moving in for the kill, he raises his gun. My sister – your brother. White eyes staring, afraid and searching.
Numbness.
BANG

The echoing silence of fighters and death. The calm after the storm and then the thunder of screams. Shock. Brave but timid they emerge from the concrete. Who, where, why and how?

Numb and naive, not knowing he stands there – waiting, watching and then he runs to the predators. Waiting, wanting, needing approval.

In his mind justice has been served.

Melinda Davis, Year 9

As mentioned earlier, this student has produced a complex narrative, but one in which the traditional structural features are not clearly evident. What is interesting about this text is the ways in which the writer has used a range of grammatical resources to create particular effects. One stark feature of her text is her play with sentence structure, such as in her use of:

- one-word sentences; for example, *Anger. Silence. Shock*
- incomplete sentences; for example, *As the vengeful brother prowls. The echoing silence of fighters and death.*

Obviously these are aspects of the grammar of narrating that should be considered once students have a good command of conventional syntax and sentence structure, but they are techniques that can be modelled and taught as a devices for narrative effect.

Another important literary technique that the writer employs is rhythm. Alliteration and the repetition of words are used throughout the text to produce a driving beat. For example, this can be seen in the following lines:

> *Searching, seeking*, honing in on the victim.
> *Slowly, silently* moving in for the kill, he raises his gun.

And also:

> Determined footsteps, *beating, beating*.

This device, occurring throughout the text, carries the narrative. In this text it operates as a type of cohesive device which aims to instil a feeling of dislocation with the themes it uses.

The aim of including this text is to encourage teachers to experiment with narrative and to move beyond what is often an overemphasis on the structural features of orientation, complication and resolution. While these are important aspects of narrative they are by no means the whole story!

TEACHING THE GENRE AND GRAMMAR OF NARRATING

TARGET GROUP: YEAR 4

SEQUENCING EVENTS

Students at this level will be competent in writing sequential texts – text types such as *recounts*. The first step, therefore, will be to use their implicit knowledge of the formal characteristics of sequencing to undertake some basic formal and functional grammatical analysis.

Base the following activity on a recent experience, such as an excursion, news (what happened on the weekend) and so on. For example,

- Have a *news* activity and ask for a volunteer to *tell* the class their news.

- Ask the class to *retell* each activity/event and scribe these on the board; for example,

  What Ryan did on the weekend
  went trampolining
  did some stretches
  put socks on
  warmed up
  practised routine
  bell rang
  started routine
  passed a level
  Mum bought him a badge.

- Explain how each of these activities/events involved something *happening* and how the word that describes the *happening* is called an *action verb*.

- Ask the class to identify the *action verb* in the first event in Ryan's news and underline it. Then go down the list, underlining each of the identified *action verbs*. For example:

  <u>went</u> trampolining
  <u>did</u> some stretches
  <u>put</u> socks on
  <u>warmed</u> up
  <u>practised</u> routine

bell <u>rang</u>
<u>started</u> routine
<u>passed</u> a level
Mum <u>**bought**</u> him a badge.

An optional activity at this point would be to discuss the tense of each of the verbs. Talk about past, present and future tenses, and how and why we use them).

- Ask the class to identify the tenses of the verbs they have identified and ask why they think all the verbs are in the past tense.

Discuss what types of words you might need to sequence all the different pieces of information from Ryan's news; for example,

- The differences between the words we use for time sequences: *then*, *when*, *after* and so on; words we use for cause and effect: *because*, *but*, *therefore* and so on; and, finally, words we use when we simply want to add one thing to another: *and*, *also*, *besides* and so on.

- Discuss why these type of words, *connectives*, are important when we want to join or connect bits of information – *clauses* and *sentences*.

Now return to the list of things that Ryan did on the weekend and ask the class to think of some connectives that could be used to join the events listed. When suggestions are made, have the class try to identify the type of connective it is.

Leave the list on the board and ask each student to write a *recount* of Ryan's news.

- Select one or two of the texts and display them on the board.

- Have the class identify the action verbs (bold) and the connectives (italicised). For example:

  On Saturday Ryan **went** trampolining at Ryde. *When* he **got** there he **did** some stretches *and* **put** his socks on. Shortly *after* that he **warmed** up *and* **practised** his routine. Time **passed**, the bell **rang** *and* he **started**. *After* his routine Ryan **passed** level four *and* his mum **bought** him a badge. Ryan was glad he **passed**.
  Adriana

- Now ask each student to draw a grid like the one below and to identify each of the action verbs and connectives they have used in their own recounts.

Action verbs	Connectives
went	When
got	and
did	after
put	and
warmed up	and
practised	After
passed	and
started	
bought	

- Discuss the structural features of these types of texts. *Recounts* normally have an *orientation*, followed by a *sequence of events*, with an optional *evaluation* stage.

  - Starting with the *orientation* stage, point out what orientations do in recounts — they indicate to the reader the people involved, the time and the place.
  - The *sequence of events* stage normally sets up a sequence of events in time and circumstance.
  - The *evaluation* stage is optional, but it normally provides some interpretation by the writer of what has happened.

- Ask the class if they can identify these stages in the texts that you have displayed on the board. For example:

On Saturday Ryan went trampolining at Ryde.	Orientation
When he got there he did some stretches and put his socks on. Shortly after that he warmed up and practised his routine. Time passed, the bell rang and he was ready to go. After his routine Ryan passed level four and his mum bought him a badge.	Sequence of events
Ryan was glad he passed.	Evaluation

THE STRUCTURE OF STORIES

Stories are more complex than simple recounts. Although stories share many of the grammatical features of recounts, they do far more than simply provide an orientation and a sequencing of events. Rather, stories create sequences in such a way as to set up a problem. The problem can then include some sort of reflection, interpretation or evaluation. Finally, the problem has to be solved, and the story normally finishes with a resolution to the problem.

- Model a simple story for the class and discuss some of the structural features of stories. For example:

The Dragon

Once there was a dragon that lived near a castle. In the castle there lived a princess with her mother and father the King and Queen.	Orientation
The dragon felt lonesome so one day when the princess went on her balcony the dragon came and kidnapped her.	Complication
The dragon saw that she was sad so when she was sleeping he gently picked her up and returned her to the castle.	Resolution

Year 1

- Ask the class to identify each of the stages of the story and then to identify individual elements within each stage. For example:

  − The orientation stage has the following elements:

Time	once in the past
Place	a castle
Characters	a dragon, a princess, her mother (the Queen) and her father (the King).

READING ACTIVITY

Use a class reading activity to further analyse a narrative for the elements of its structure.

- Read a story to the class (a big book, or a class set of books, is ideal for this activity). Ask the class to identify where the story moves from the orientation stage on to the complication stage. For example, in the big book of the story *Baleen the Whale*, the elements of the orientation are:

Time	once upon a time
Place	the sea
Character	Baleen, a greedy whale.

- The elements of the complication stage are:
  - Baleen had a bone in his throat
  - Baleen attacked Bluntt
  - attacking Bluntt was against the rules.

- The elements of the resolution stage are:
  - Bluntt saved Baleen
  - Baleen changed.

IDENTIFYING THE THEME OF A STORY

Discuss the idea of *theme* with the class. Explain how the *theme* of a story is its main idea or message. For example, in a story such as *Baleen*, which is a myth, the main message operates on two levels: first, it offers an account of the reason for baleen whales having a bone-like structure rather than teeth, hanging from their upper jaw. At another level, the myth provides a moral for socially acceptable human behaviour – that greed, violence, selfishness and breaking the rules of a society will ultimately fail.

- Ask the class to identify the *theme* or main message of the *Baleen* story.

- Think of other stories that the class has read and have the students identify the *themes* of each.

SCAFFOLDING A STORY USING THE GENERIC STRUCTURE AND THEME

Using the following scaffold as an OHT or as a handout, brainstorm with the class for ideas for the framework of a story.

- Start with the *theme* and discuss what sort of main message the story will have. In the following example, the students loosely modelled their own story on the *Baleen* story they had recently read.

- Point out how each of the categories is interconnected. For example, the characters should exemplify and contrast the issues in the theme. Or, the complication stage should be planned to lead into the resolution.

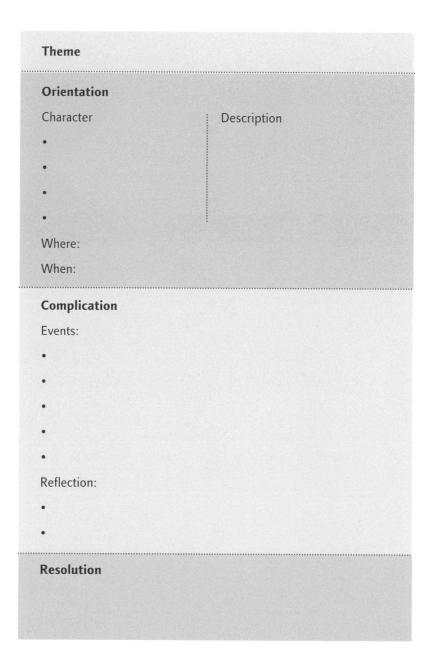

Theme

Orientation

Character	Description
•	
•	
•	
•	

Where:

When:

Complication

Events:

- •
- •
- •
- •
- •

Reflection:

- •
- •

Resolution

WRITING INDIVIDUAL NARRATIVES

Ask the students in the class to develop their own story plans, based on the above activity. Expect to see similarities in their plans and a similar theme to the one in the story you have analysed in the reading activity. Remember that the aim here is to provide students with a model for planning stories.

• Compare and contrast two or three of the story plans and discuss the different elements that have been used in each stage of the story. For example,

Theme	Don't take more than you need
Orientation	
Character	*Description*
Pig	– greedy
Horse	– generous
Mr and Mrs Smith	– poor farmers
Where	Barn yard
When	In the past
Complication	
Events	• Pig ate too much
	• Pig wouldn't share with other animals
	• Pig gets sick
	• The farmers call the vet
	• The vet warns him he could die
Reflection	•
	•
Resolution	
The horse and the other animals help him. He gets better and stops being greedy.	

The students in the class should now be ready to write their own stories. Take time to ensure that the class understands how the events in the *complication* stage need to set up a solution to the problem they have created. It may be necessary to assist students individually with this.

• Once students have written their stories, compare and contrast some examples and have the class identify the structural and grammatical features of each.

A long time ago there was a barn with owners named Mr and Mrs Smith. They were poor and they only had a horse for riding, 2 sheep for wool,1 pig and a bull and a cow for milk.

They were poor because their pig ate them out of house and home and he didn't share with the other animals. His name was Bob. 'You should go on a diet' said Clarabelle the horse. 'Oh be quiet, I'm not fat I've got big bones'. A few minutes later Bob was rolling around on the ground. 'I'm sick, I'm sick', he shouted. 'Help me, help me'. Mr and Mrs Smith ran down and called the vet. The vet came quickly and said quietly, 'If he eats like he has been eating he'll surely die'. 'Oh', groaned the pig.

Clarabelle overheard and said to the other animals, 'Our friend is dying, we've got to help him'. 'Yeh' said the other animals 'lets go'. They went up to Bob and said, 'We are going to get you in shape'. First they told him to eat only half of the food in the trof. Then they made him run up and down the hill and made him swim in the duck pond.

He did this every day for three long weeks and he got better and he thanked Clarabelle and Bob was never greedy again.

Erin, Year 4

ASSESSING TEXTS USING THE GENRE OF NARRATING: A RECOUNT

The following writing task asked Year 6 students to write a descriptive recount based on visual and verbal stimulus material of a recent newsworthy event. Their text needed to emphasise the drama and danger of the situation and they were given the key features of the genre and a suitable model.

Your local newspaper regularly prints articles about people who have survived dangerous situations. In the articles, the facts are presented in a dramatic way to provide information and recreate the dangers these people faced. The feelings and reactions of the survivor are also described.

You have been asked to write an article about Richard Van Pham. Information about what happened to Mr Pham is provided below.

Name
• Richard Van Pham

Place
• Pacific Ocean, off the west coast of the United States of America

Time at sea
- 4 months

Events
- left Long Beach, California, to sail 35 kilometres to Catalina Island
- yacht's mast broke in a storm
- motor and radio both stopped working
- drifted 4000 kilometres to Costa Rica
- ate fish and seabirds and drank rainwater
- found by US navy ship after 4 months alone at sea

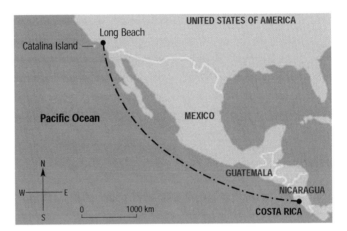

The following are the assessment criteria used for assessing the task based on the appropriate generic structural and grammatical features described earlier in this chapter.

1 *Genre-based* criteria deal with the macro level features of the text. This level covers the first six criteria:

- does the text mainly recount and/or use setting and characterisation to enhance the recount?
- is the theme of the writing consistent with the task?
- is the writing well organised and does it include an introduction, a sequence and a conclusion?
- does the writing use appropriate generic strategies such as direct or reported speech, passive voice, nominalisation and technical language?
- does the writing use affective/reflective language such as reflective comments and language designed to have an emotive effect on the reader?
- are other descriptive devices used such as adjectives?

2 *Textual language* criteria deal with the way that the text is held together, the way that sentences are structured and how sentences work with one another. This level covers the next five criteria:
  - is the recount organised in logical and/or meaningful paragraphs?
  - does the text use a range of simple, compound and complex sentence structures?
  - is the choice of tense appropriate and consistently maintained?
  - is appropriate reference maintained through the use of pronouns?
  - does the text make appropriate use of a variety of connectives?

3 *Syntactical language* criteria deal with the internal structure of the sentences used. This level covers the next criteria:
  - do the sentences have essential elements such as a main verb and do statements have the subject and main verb in the correct order?
  - do the subject and main verb agree in person and number?
  - are prepositions used appropriately?
  - are articles used correctly in every instance?
  - is simple and complex punctuation correct?

4 *Spelling* deals with the way that individual words across the text are spelt. This level comprises the following criteria:
  - are most high-frequency words spelt correctly?
  - are most less frequently used words and words with common but not simple patterns spelt correctly?
  - are most words with difficult or unusual patterns spelt correctly?
  - are most challenging words appropriate to the task spelt correctly?
  - are all challenging words appropriate to the task spelt correctly?

The Rescue of Richard Van Pham

1 On the seventeenth of September Richard Van Pham
  was rescued by the U.S Navy.
  It was a nice sunny day when Van Pham took his boat
  out and go to Catalina Island off the west coast of
5 the United States when suddenly a strong wind hit
  when Van Pham had just left the bay. The wind was
  too strong so he could'nt turn back. So he kept going
  on until a storm hit and his mast broke off and fell into the
  water. Then Van Pham's motor and radio both failed.
10 Richard survived on fish, seabirds and rainwater while drifting

4000 km to Costa Rica. After four months alone at
sea, a U,S navy ship found Van Pham.
Richard's family told the media they where glad
that he was home.

Year 6

GENRE

GENRE AND THEME

The writing mainly recounts, but there is too little depth in the
account for the text to be dramatic.

The theme is consistent and stays on the task.

TEXT STRUCTURE

The writing begins with a basic introduction, there is a sequence of
events and the family's comments are used as a conclusion.

GENERIC STRATEGIES

The writing uses indirect speech 9l. 13–14) and passive voice (l. 2).
Only two temporal connectives are used: l. 1 *On* the seventeenth of
September ..., l. 11 *After* four months ...

REFLECTIVE/AFFECTIVE LANGUAGE

There is only a limited example of reflective/affective language such
as the reflective comment (l. 3 *It was a nice sunny day* ...).

DESCRIPTIVE LANGUAGE

There is only basic descriptive language used (l. 5 *suddenly a strong wind hit*).

TEXTUAL LANGUAGE

PARAGRAPHS

Some paragraphs are indicated although they are not always logical.

SENTENCE STRUCTURE

Almost all sentences are correctly structured and four sentences
have dependent clauses (l. 6 *The wind was too strong* ..., l. 10 *Richard
survived on fish* ... l. 11 *After four months at sea* ... l. 13 *Richard's
family told* ...). The second sentence, however, is too long, overly
complex and lacks cohesion.

TENSE

Tense is generally consistent, although there is the use of incorrect tense in l. 4 *Van Pham took his boat out and go [went] to sea.*

PRONOUNS

Pronouns are used correctly throughout the text, although there is an illogical switch from Van Pham to Richard (l. 10, l. 13).

CONNECTIVES

Most connectives are used correctly and appropriately, although *when* is used incorrectly (l. 5) and repetitively.

SYNTACTICAL LANGUAGE

CLAUSE PATTERN

Sentences always have a main clause and all finite clauses have a subject and finite verb.

AGREEMENT

All verb forms agree with their subjects.

ARTICLES

All articles and plurals are correct.

PUNCTUATION

All sentence punctuation is correct, but there are two errors in simple punctuation: l. 2 and 12 *U.S* and l. 7 *could'nt.*

SPELLING

Most less frequently used words and words with common but not simple patterns are spelt correctly, but there is confusion with the correct spelling of the homophones *where (were).*

SUMMARY

This text demonstrates a basic understanding of the genre by following the task and model, and it demonstrates a elementary understanding of the structure for the genre. The writing narrates but does not dramatise the character or setting. The writing demonstrates a suitable level of sentence structure and syntax, although one of the complex sentences is poorly structured. Most less-frequently used words are spelt correctly, although there is confusion with the spelling of a homophone. Most sentence and simple punctuation is correct.

STRATEGIES TO IMPROVE THE USE OF AFFECTIVE LANGUAGE

This writer's limited use of affective language is not uncommon. As a rule, students are far less successful at using affective verbs and adverbs than they are at using affective noun groups and adjectives.

• First discuss the various roles of descriptive language in writing. For example, some words are used to provide extra information about nouns or things – words like small car, yellow bus, angry penguin and so on. Point out that these words are called adjectives. Adjectives such as these can be referred to as common or neutral because they provide basic everyday information about the nouns they modify.

• Now discuss how adjectives can be used for other purposes. For example, in factual writing adjectives are often used to provide technical information about nouns; words such as _igneous_ rocks, _hexagonal_ columns, _superficial_ corrosion and so on.

• Finally, adjectives can be used to affect readers in some way, such as _monstrous_ problem, _exquisite_ jewel, _maddening_ person and so on. These words can be called affective adjectives and they are common in narrative writing or writing that aims to have an effect on its readers.

• As a class activity, display examples of each of the above types of noun groups and with the class identify the adjectives used. For example,

large house	Common
subterranean structure	Technical
spectacular vision	Affective

• As an individual or group activity have students identify the common or neutral adjectives in the following text and where appropriate replace them with affective adjectives.

It was a *big* day out. My brother was *happy* that we were invited. There was a *big* picnic lunch which had lots of junk food. Our mother thought it was a *nice* lunch but was worried we would eat too much. After lunch we had a *lovely* swim to cool down because it was such a *hot* day. Finally we went home in our *old* car and we all fell asleep.

- Now discuss how verbs can be similarly used to have an affective function in writing. With the class, compare and contrast the following sentences.

  We slowly *walked down* to the cave.
  We slowly *descended* into the cave.

Point out how affective verbs can be used to give readers a feeling for what is being described in the writing.

- Discuss how the role of adverbs is to provide extra information about verbs and adjectives. When used carefully, adverbs can enhance their effectiveness. For example,

an exquisitely beautiful jewel	Modifying an adjective
the dog whined pathetically	Modifying a verb

- As a class or individual activity have students identify the affective verbs and adverbs in the following passage and discuss their effect.

  She hated the wind, the way it *hurled* itself at her in *raw* gusts of heat. She hated the grasshoppers humming *hoarsely* out of the grass. She hated the cicadas, the *pressure-waves of drilling* that felt as if a blood vessel in your head was about to burst. She hated the dog, trotting now in front, now behind, panting noisily. She could not bear to look at its tongue, red and *desperate*, hanging out, drying.

  She despised the look of the *depressingly* dirty terminal. The way that the vendors *insolently* hurled themselves at you *thrusting* their cheap imitation watches and jewellery into your face. What was worse, she knew that the minute they stepped outside they would *swelter* in the *oppressively insistent* heat.

  K. Grenville (1999) *The Idea of Perfection*,
  South Melbourne, Picador, p. 341.

STRATEGIES TO ASSIST WRITERS SHIFTING TENSE IN TEXTS THAT NARRATE

The following activities focus on providing students with knowledge and strategies for effectively shifting tense where appropriate in a narrative text. For activities that focus on providing students with basic information on the form and function of tense, see page 67.

• Point out that narrative writing that is recounting or recalling past events is written in the past tense. For example,

> The silence *was* excruciating. Not a thing *moved*, not a floorboard *creaked*. The noiselessness *covered* them like a thick, cotton quilt.

> The heat *was* unbearable. Beads of perspiration *dripped* down Nick's cheeks like a waterfall.

• As a class activity display a passage from a narrative text and jointly identify the verbs and their tense. For example,

> Old and musty time *was* in every object. Christopher *had discovered* the wonders in his dimly lit attic. He *was* only seven but he <u>had</u> an amazing imagination. He *could fly* planes and *battle* gangsters without *leaving* (non-finite) his bedroom. Now he *had hit* upon a goldmine of props for his adventures.

• Ask the class why this passage has been written in the past tense. Following this, point out that narratives often make shifts in tense depending on what the narrator is doing with the story. For example, if the narrator wants to make a comment on the action taking place then the tense will shift to the present and then revert to the past tense when it returns to the action. For example,

> There *is* something suspicious about the way that he *goes* about his business. Yesterday he **arrived** home later than usual. He **climbed** the stairs and **went** straight to his room and **didn't emerge** until late in the night. Now this *seems* to me to be like he *is trying* to conceal something.

• Point out how the tense shifts as the narrative moves from present tense when the narrator addresses the reader in the first and fourth sentences to past tense when the narrator recounts events in the second and third sentences.

- As an individual activity have the students write their own narratives where they insert commentary on events. Then have them identify the tense of the verbs they have used.

SPELLING

While students have successfully spelt most of the words attempted in the text, the level of difficult words attempted is not particularly high. The following strategies are designed to assist students to attempt vocabulary with more difficult spelling patterns in their writing.

Many students experience difficulties correctly spelling common words which do not have simple patterns such as *kn*, *wh*, *ey*, *ou*, *au*, *ould*, *ous*, *dge*, *ie*, *ough* and *ought*, and adding suffixes to words ending in *e, c,* or *l*. For example, the following are typical of those words causing problems: *health, through, friend, struggling, rescuers, energy, plastic, where/wear, easier, strength, cause, really, sustain, defend, branches, dangerous, pathway, sure, group* and *should*.

- Discuss the silent 'k' in the consonant sound 'n'. Point out that most words starting with the 'n' consonant do not have a silent 'k', although there are many words that do. Brainstorm for as many words that have a silent 'k'. For example,

knee	knew	know	knowledge
knot	knelt	knit	knock
knight	knuckle	knack	kneel
knapsack	knob	knead	knickers
knoll	knave	knife	known

- As an individual activity, have students write their own sentences using words from the brainstormed list.

- Conduct a similar activity with the consonant sound 'wh', including words that begin with the sound and words that contain the sound. For example,

when	what	which	whether
where	white	while	why
wheat	whale	whip	whisper
whistle	wharf	whiff	awhile
overwhelm	somewhat	everywhere	meanwhile
buckwheat	cartwheel	somewhere	anywhere

- Again have students write their own sentences from the list of these words.

- Other activities can be conducted using other problematic digraphs (two-letter blends) and phonograms (a cluster of letters with a stable pronunciation that forms part of a word).

EA vowel sound: long E

eat	each	east	easy
eagle	eager	easel	ease
neat	read	least	beat
clean	deal	leaf	meat
deal	feast	peach	flea

EA vowel sound: short E

head	health	ready	thread
steady	dead	breath	deaf
breakfast	feather	measure	instead
measure	leather	meadow	spread
sweat	treasure	weapon	weather

OU vowel sound

out	our	ounce	ouch
outside	ourselves	hour	sound
about			
around	scout	amount	aloud
found	council	ground	loud
cloud	doubt	count	

AU vowel sound

August	author	autumn	auditorium
autograph	audience	auction	auburn
auxiliary	automatic	audible	authentic
because	caught	laundry	haul
daughter	fault	cause	dinosaur
sauce	caution	exhaust	fraud
launch	overhaul		

OULD phonogram

could	would	should

OUGH phonogram

rough	tough	enough

OUGHT phonogram

bought	fought	ought	sought
brought	thought		

Finally, after completing these activities have students attempt a similar task and compare with the first text.

Bibliography

Austin, J.L. (1962) *How to Do Things with Words*, Oxford: Oxford University Press.

Bakhtin, M.M. (1952) *Speech Genres and Other Late Essays*, ed. by C. Emerson and M. Holquist, trans. by V.M. McGee, Austin TX: University of Texas Press.

Barnes,D., Britton, J. and Rosen, M. (1971) *Language, the Learner and the School*, London: Penguin.

Bourdieu, P. (1990) *The Logic of Practice*, trans. Richard Nice, Stanford CA: Stanford University Press.

Bourdieu, P. (2000) *Pascalian Meditations*, trans. R. Nice. Cambridge: Polity Press.

Callaghan, M., Knapp, P. and Noble, G. (1993) 'Genre in Practice', in B. Cope and M. Kalantzis (eds), *The Powers of Literacy: A Genre Approach to Teaching Writing*, The Falmer Press: London.

Callaghan, M. and Rothery J. (1988) *Teaching Factual Writing: A Genre-based Approach*, Erskineville: Metropolitan East Disadvantaged Schools Program, New South Wales Department of Education.

Cambourne, B. (1988) *The Whole Story: Natural Learning and the Acquisition of Literacy in the Classroom*, Auckland: Ashton Scholarship.

Chomsky, N. (1965) *Aspects of the Theory of Syntax*, Cambridge, Mass: MIT Press.

Cope, B., Kalantzis, M., Kress, G., Martin, J. and Murphy, L. (1993) 'Bibliographical Essay: Developing the Theory and Practice of Genre-based Literacy', in B. Cope and M. Kalantzis (eds), *The Powers of Literacy – A Genre Approach to Teaching Literacy*, London: The Falmer Press.

Derewianka, B. (1990) *Exploring How Texts Work*, Sydney: PETA.

Dixon, J. (1967) *Growth through English*, Yorkshire: National Association for the

Teaching of English.

Fowler, R. and Kress, G. (1979) 'Rules and Regulations', in R. Fowler, B. Hodge, G. Kress and T. Trew (eds), *Language and Control*, London: Routledge and Kegan Paul.

Freadman, A. (1987) 'Anyone for Tennis?', in Ian Reid (ed.) *The Place of Genre in Learning: Current Debates*, Geelong: Deakin University, Centre for Studies in Literary Education.

Freadman, A. (1994) *Models of Genre for Language Teaching*, Sonia Marks Memorial Lecture, Sydney University, 13 October 1994.

Freadman, A. and Macdonald, A. (1992) *What is this Thing Called 'Genre'?*, Brisbane: Boombana Publications.

Freedman, A (1994) 'Do as I Say': The Relationship between Teaching and Learning New Genres, in A Freedman and P. Medway (eds) *Genre and the New Rhetoric*, London: Taylor and Francis.

Goodman, K. (1986) *What's Whole in Whole Language?*, Portsmouth NH: Heinemann.

Graves, D.H. (1975) 'An Examination of the Writing Processes of Seven-year-old Children', *Research in the Teaching of English*, 9:227–41.

Graves, D.H. (1978) *Balance the Basics: Let Them Write*, New York: Ford Foundation.

Graves, D.H. (1983) *Writing: Teachers and Children at Work*, Exeter, NH: Heinemann Educational Books.

Halliday, M.A.K. (1975) *Learning to Mean – Explorations in the Development of Language*, London: Edward Arnold.

Halliday, M.A.K. (1978) *Language as Social Semiotic: The Social Interpretation of Language and Meaning*, London: Edward Arnold.

Halliday, M.A.K. (1985) *An Introduction to Functional Grammar*, London: Edward Arnold.

Hammond, J. (1991) 'Is Learning to Read and Write the Same as Learning to Speak?', in F. Christie (ed.) *Literacy for a Changing World*, Hawthorn, Victoria: ACER Press.

Hammond, J. (2001) 'Scaffolding and Language', in J. Hammond (ed), *Teaching and Learning in Language and Literacy Education*, Newtown, NSW: PETA.

Hjelmslev, L. (1961) *Prolegomena to a Theory of Language*, trans. by Francis J. Whitfield, revised English edition, Madison and London: University of Wisconsin Press.

Hodge, R. and Kress, G. (1993) *Language as Ideology*, London: Routledge and Kegan Paul.

Johns, A. (2002) Introduction in A. Johns, *Genre in the Classroom – Multiple Perspectives*, Mahwah, NJ: Lawrence Erlbaum.

Klein, R. (1983) *Junk Castle*, Melbourne: Oxford University Press.

Knapp, P. (1989) 'The Politics of Process', *Education*, 70:4.

Knapp, P. (1992) *Resource Book for Genre and Grammar*, Metropolitan West Literacy and Learning Program, Parramatta: NSW Dept of School Education.

Knapp, P. and Watkins, M. (1994) *Context–Text–Grammar: Teaching the Genres and Grammar of School Writing in Infants and Primary Classrooms*, Broadway: Text Productions.

Krashen, S.D. (1981) *Second Language Acquisition and Second Language Learning*, Oxford: Pergamon Press.

Krashen, S.D. (1984) *Writing: Research, Theory and Applications*, Oxford: Pergamon Press.

Kress, G.R. (1979) 'The Social Values of Speech and Writing', in *Language and Control*, Roger Fowler, Bob Hodge, Gunther Kress and Tony Trew (eds), London: Routledge and Kegan Paul.

Kress, G.R. (1982) *Learning to Write*, London: Routledge and Kegan Paul.

Kress, G.R. (1985) *Linguistic Processes in Sociocultural Practice*, Geelong: Deakin University Press.

Kress, G. (1989) 'Texture and Meaning', in R. Andrews (ed.) *Narrative and Argument*,

Milton Keynes: Open University Press.

Kress, G. and Knapp P. (1992) 'Genre in a Social Theory of Language', *English in Education* (UK), 20, 2.

Kress, G. (1993) 'Genre as Social Process', in B. Cope and M. Kalantzis (eds), *The Powers of Literacy – A Genre Approach to Teaching Literacy*, London: The Falmer Press.

Lee, A. (1993) 'Whose Geography? A Feminist-postructuralist Critique of Systemic Genre-base Accounts of Literacy and Curriculum', *Social Semiotics*, 3, 1:131–56.

Luke, A (1994) 'Genres of Power? Literacy Education and thge Production of Capital', in Hasan, R.and Williams, G (eds) Literacy and Society, London: Longman.

Malinowski, B. (1967) *A Diary in the Strict Sense of the Term*, London: Routledge.

Martin, J.R. (1986) 'Systemic Functional Linguistics and an Understanding of Written Text', in *Writing Project—Report 1986, Working Papers in Linguistics 4*, Department of Linguistics: University of Sydney.

Martin, J.R. (1987) *Writing Project Report No. 5,* Department of Linguistics, University of Sydney.

Martin, J.R. (1992) *English Text – System and Structure*. Philadelphia: John Benjamin.

Martin, J.R. and Rothery, J. (1993) Grammar – Making Meaning in Writing in B. Cope and M. Kalantzis (eds), *The Powers of Literacy – A Genre Approach to Teaching Literacy*, London: The Falmer Press.

New South Wales Department of Education (1974) *Curriculum for Primary Schools: Language*, Sydney: Government Printer.

New South Wales Department of Education and Training (2003) *Quality Teaching in NSW Public Schools – Discussion Paper*, Sydney: New South Wales Department of Education and Training.

Painter, C. (1991) *Learning the Mother Tongue*, Geelong: Deakin University Press.

Poynton, C. (1993) 'Grammar, Language and the Social: Postructuralism and Systemic Functional Linguistics', *Social Semiotics*, 3, 1:41–6.

Reid, I. (ed.) (1987) *The Place of Genre in Learning: Current Debates*, Geelong: Deakin University Press.

Richardson, P. (1991) 'Language as Personal Response and as Social Construct – Competing Literacy Pedagogies in Australia', *Educational Review*, 43, 2.

Rothery, J. (1986) 'Teaching Genre in the Primary School: A Genre-based Approach to the Development of Writing Abilities', *Writing Project Report. Working Papers in Linguistics 4,* Department of Linguistics. University of Sydney, pp. 3–62.

Saussure, F. de (1974) *Course in General Linguistics*, trans. R. Harris, Bungay, Suffolk: Fontana.

Smith, F. (1975) Comprehension and Learning: A Conceptual Framework for Teachers, New York: Holt, Rinehart and Winston.

Smith, F. (1983) 'Reading Like a Writer', *Language Arts*, 60, 5, pp. 558–67.

Threadgold, T. (1992) 'Legislators and Interpreters: Linguists, Feminists and Critical Fictions', *Meridian*, 11, 1:76–91.

Threadgold, T. (1993) 'Violence, The Making of Protected Subjects, and the Discourses of Critical Literacy and Radical Pedagogy', *Changing English*, 1, 1:2–31.

Threadgold, T (1994) 'Grammar, Genre and the Ownership of Literacy', *Idiom*, 2:20–8.

Van der Veer, R. and Valsiner, J. (1991) *Understanding Vygotsky: A Quest for Synthesis*, Oxford: Blackwell.

Vygotsky, L. (1996) *Thought and Language*, Cambridge, Massachusetts: The MIT Press.

Walshe, R.D. (1981a) *Don Graves in Australia – Children Want to Write*, Rozelle: Primary English Teaching Association.

Walshe, R.D. (1981b) *Every Child Can Write*, Rozelle: Primary English Teaching Association.

Watkins, M. (1990) 'A Cry for Help Unanswered', *Education Australia*, 7.

Watkins, M. (1997) 'Textual Recipes: Language Pedagogy and Classroom Discourse', *Southern Review*, 30, 3, pp. 287–301.

Watkins, M. (1999) 'Policing the Text: Structuralism's Stranglehold on Australian Language and Literacy Pedagogy', *Language and Education*, 13, 2, pp. 118–132.

Watkins, M. and Knapp, P. (1998) *Far Out – Connecting Text and Grammar*, Alexandria: Blake Education.

Williams, G. (1993) 'Using Systemic Grammar in Teaching Young Learners: An Introduction', in L. Unsworth (ed.) *Literacy, Learning and Teaching Language as Social Practice in Primary School*. South Melbourne: MacMillan.

Wittgenstein, L. (1953) *Philosophical Investigations*, trans. by G.E.M. Anscombe, Oxford: Basil Blackwell.

Index

References to figures are in *italics*.